AM I REALLY A CHRISTIAN?

James E. Kifer

New Harbor Press
RAPID CITY, SD

Kifer/New Harbor Press
1601 Mt. Rushmore Rd., Ste 3288
Rapid City, SD 57701
www.NewHarborPress.com

Ordering Information:
Quantity sales. Special discounts are available on quantity purchases by corporations, associations, and others. For details, contact the "Special Sales Department" at the address above.

Am I Really a Christian? / James E. Kifer. -- 1st ed.
ISBN 978-1-63357-480-9

Contents

PREFACE

Am I really a Christian? Admittedly, this is a strange, even perplexing, title for a book the primary audience of which is Christian, in many cases Christians of a lifelong tenure in the faith. The reflexive answer of that person is apt to be "of course," but a central premise of this work is that a shockingly large percentage of publicly identifying Christians are individuals who harbor, fearfully and ominously, a feeling that in reality maybe they have missed the mark and are not counted among the faithful and the saved, or in perhaps Christ's most frequently employed metaphorical example, are "members of the flock."

The author has conceded and aggregated to himself the right to claim membership in this surprisingly large flock of men and women who have and in some or sadly perhaps most cases remain plagued by self-doubts as to their own merits, self-worth and legitimacy as disciples of the Savior, Jesus Christ. I will with intention limit most, if not all, my personal references and examples to this brief Preface; however, on such an intricate issue as salvation and self-doubt at least a bit of personal example and observation is necessary. This will not be an extended essay on what many have called the "plan of salvation," that process of belief, repentance, confession and baptism, which is so plainly set forth and endlessly but simply taught in the New Testament. Rather my hopes and intentions are to focus upon the fears, the worries, the self-doubts and the plain mental torture that has often been inflicted by Christians upon themselves (and often upon fellow Christians) in an effort to determine whether our answer to the titular question is actually a "yes."

After a life of three quarters of a century I recall and now understand in greater depth the fortuitous circumstances of my birth, childhood and youth, all of which I hope and believe remain highly influential in my life, personal relationships and beliefs. My birth naturally uncelebrated by the world, occurred precisely in mid-twentieth century small town America in what many sophisticates have sneeringly referenced as the Bible Belt. Far more important than time or place, though, were people. My parents, of impeccable character and reputation, were of what gradually became called the Greatest Generation, although that was a term unknown to me (and to them) during my childhood and youth. This was the American generation which had suffered the seemingly endless economic fears and scourge of the Great Depression, only to see it end by the conflagration of World War II, in which my father played a role and in which, as with so many, my family's lives were pummeled by upheaval.

The post war period was a time of building in the United States, and the "building" seemed to be all encompassing. Cities, industries and commerce, expanded families grew so noticeably that the terminology of description remains to the present. My own birth was a part of the "boom," the Baby Boom, and by the appellation of Boomer my generation is known yet today. With the proliferation of "Boomers" came the building of so many other edifices, real and concrete but in the most important ways spiritual and esoteric. The post-war period, probably for these purposes, lasting through the 1960's, witnessed a growth of churches, church membership, and church-related activities unseen since the Great Awakening of the early 1800's. Families were being constructed and with them came an interest in the Christian religion as never before in modern times. Statistics are readily available for those who delight in numbers, but all Christian identified groups, be they Roman Catholic, Eastern Orthodox and the kaleidoscopic array of Protestant bodies grew at a steady pace. As a personal aside I grew hearing the constant refrain that my own church, the Church of Christ, was the fastest growing church in the United States. Actually, I never saw any verifiable numbers one way or another on that contention. Whether true or not my church was growing, as were most, if not all the churches, of my friends and acquaintances.

From the onset of life I was blessed not only with exemplary parents, who were no more perfect than other mortals, always made God and His will and judgment the center of their thinking and the lodestar of the moral arcs of their lives. At church, especially in the early childhood years, I enjoyed the benefits of mostly good, often excellent teachers, and in the main, but not exclusively, women. Almost from infancy I was raised in the surroundings of the stories and precepts of the Biblical canon and the Christian morality to which I attempt to adhere. With the hope of not falling into triteness of expression my moral upbringing was permeated with the code of "good is good" and "bad," while deplorable is always something I should change in myself. Although the word seems alien to the demands of modernistic frenzy it was an "idyllic" time and place, the enjoyments of which were given not only to myself but to many of my companions of the time and of the era.

Even spiritually, though, it was not a time of perfection, and in the mass of moral principles taught to us and even more importantly so demonstrated by our teachers, parents, elders and superiors was an almost spoken (though customarily tacit) instruction that if not everything, most things depended upon our own efforts. In good conscience and without lapsing into outright hypocrisy I cannot argue with the basic truth of that statement. That one life (each's own) which is entrusted into our own hands of care is in great measure what we determine it to be. Certainly, only a very myopic and foolish person would deny that all persons are born with certain advantages and disadvantages which are proprietary to themselves. Only a few have the innate talent for genuine artistry, to be a skilled surgeon or a technological genius. Fewer still possess the ability to save their own souls. In fact the fewer should be rendered as the number zero. Many, including, perhaps even especially myself, without sufficient understanding and self-knowledge were gradually captured by a generally unspoken doctrine that eternal spiritual salvation depends upon our own personal efforts. "Work for the night is coming..." were the clarion words of an old hymn, or another similar reading "We'll work till Jesus comes..." or more prosaically, almost verging upon a threatening spiritual brutality, is a common Christian refrain/encouragement/threat to a new Christian that "... we will put you to work" or "now the real work begins." It is not we in the Church of Christ only, though, that were steadily with both directness and a type of spiritual osmosis, that emphasized works above all. For centuries the most visible and noted denomination in Christendom has been the Roman Catholic church, whose teachings traditionally have placed a heavy emphasis upon works. None of these observations is intended to denigrate the essential importance of works to the Christian faith and life, and in actuality the opposite is true. Too many of us Christians, though, with the best intentions, were not so thoroughly that our personal efforts, deeds of goodness, benevolence and morality were so central to the acceptable Christian life that many Christians, consciously or not, were and still remain striving to secure the personal salvation which was vouchsafed to them not by their own merits but by the blood of Christ and the grace of God. In the most practical terms I have seen good Christians become discouraged to the point of apostasy or continued unhappy in their faith because they had "never done enough." The author would not be penning these words unless he himself had often so shared in these sentiments.

These are attitudes which were larcenous of the true scarcity of believers, of faithful disciples, of determined admirable Christians, and often robbed them not of their own peace that passes understanding. I recall, still with vivid memories, the funeral of my own grandfather in January 1969. He was a good man, a lifelong Christian of faith, and of course, by no means a perfect man. The minister officiating at his service in a small Oklahoma town made a remark that lives with me yet, and in fact, the only moment from the service which I remember. "Shame on us," he intoned "shame on us if we 'preach' this man into Heaven, for we do not know, and it is God's decision alone." The latter portion of the expression is one in which no disagreement may be offered, for of course, it is God's decision. Yet God proclaimed to the universe that those who follow His Son Christ are saved. Both testaments from Creation to Revelation are tied by the spine of the Great Story, that of how God redeemed the fallen through the sacrifice of His Son. Shame on us, yes. Shame on us if we as Christians still reject the security of the believer's salvation. In a zeal, not necessarily misplaced, not to usurp God's authority many Christians have hardened their thinking resulting in a real lack of respect for the power and the grace of God.

Other funeral examples could be offered, many based upon the author's personal knowledge, but let us proceed to other of the manifestations of this lack of faith. With my own ears often have I heard some of the finest men and women I have known remark plaintively and a bit apprehensively that "I hope that I am saved." We are to pity lifelong Christians, dedicated to living righteously, who approach the thoughts of "eternity" with merely a hope. So many Biblical examples to the contrary may be furnished. David finished his 23rd Psalm, perhaps the most famous poem ever written, where this great king and writer who lived over a millennium before Christ spoke that "I shall dwell in the House of the Lord forever." Absolutely no doubt there.

Such fretful worries as have been presented are to be expected in children and youth, those same persons who are new to the Christian faith and as yet unaware of the power, patience and grace of God. One is reminded of the admirable young man who happily came to Christ, he who was a young man already possessed of great accomplishment, being a "ruler" or official in the Temple. He fairly bounded to Jesus and inquired what he yet lacked to secure his own salvation. The Master reminded him of the basic moral commandments of the Law, its teachings about reverence to God and love to his fellow men. Gladly, perhaps even excitedly, this accomplished young man replied to the Master that he had always scrupulously kept the Law and lived a morally exemplary life. "What lack I yet?" he asked Jesus, who shocked him with the reply that he should dispose of all his property, donate the proceeds to the poor and follow Christ. The youth, a man greatly loved by Jesus, turned away with tragic disappointment and walked from the Master. Christ's apostles were nonplussed in their reactions and exclaimed that if such moral stricture and upright behavior did not merit salvation and Heaven "... who then could be saved?" Not works, Jesus replied, but it was faith and devotion to Christ Himself for which He was seeking.

The "rich young ruler," as he has been labeled has a biography that meets more than a few persons which the author himself has known. They are good persons, good Christians who do much good, all of which is highly laudatory. They work hard in their Christianity, ever striving to do more and to be better, apparently not cognizant of the centrality of truth that not a single nor multiple set of good works is any currency in the purchase of even one day's heavenly reward. All their efforts are to be applauded, their multitude of good works laudatory, and their characters exemplary. Yet it is impossible that even a single good work moves the needle of salvation any closer to its goal. A lifetime of these efforts should be extolled, but simultaneously it may wear on the psyche and the soul. Too often the drive to "do good" in the Church is accompanied by its fellow emotion that chastises and torments the faithful Christian with the query of "... am I doing enough," which is a robber of the blessed assurance of salvation. Salvation comes not from works but rather from obedience to Christ. Sometimes and with many Christians, they become tormented with the belief that salvation is just beyond the reach of their stretching fingers, which itself is germanous to other questions. Can I ever do enough to be saved, and our titular heading Am I Really a Christian? The answer to the former question is yes in that no one has ever done enough to secure salvation. The simple corollary is that all Christians are incapable of earning by work even a brief moment of salvation. We do not have the spiritual wherewithal of self-salvation by works. Not only that, but this attitude of constantly working, continually seeking to improve ourselves is likely to be ultimately discouraging and actually harmful to a desire to do good works. Should a Christian seek salvation from works he is the traveler whose eyes are not fixed upon a life-giving oasis but rather upon a cruel mirage. Eventually many Christians, including and especially those of the author's generation are like the rich young ruler who became discouraged but "... went away sorrowful." The young man as well as Christians for two millennia since have shown brightly with good works and good character, but a certainty of salvation has never been located, nor will it ever be found in any of our works. One last reference to the young man of Christ's encounter – Christ's own disciples were astonished and inquired if a man such as this is not saved who then can be saved. Jesus answered that with His Father all things were possible, and herein is found that the possibility lies in Christ and in Christ alone.

It is a tragedy of the first order that many good Christians lead strong, faithful, spiritually rich lives and still carry the baggage of doubt about their own salvation. They have been robbed of years of confidence, which itself, when maintained within its proper boundaries, may be an engine driving spiritual growth. In so many instances there should be the very spiritual exemplars whose wisdom and spiritual contentment has long been mortgaged to self-doubt. The faithful Christian soul should be filled not with self-doubt, insecurity and a sense of ongoing failure but rather with joy, peace, comfort and security. Too often the former, though, has been more common than the latter. The Christian believes and teaches that the coming of Jesus Christ and the founding of Christianity are the greatest manifestations and reasons for ecstasy and joy the world has ever known, yet we plague ourselves with self-doubt and spiritually self-immolation. How can this be?

A child, be they of any age, who is uncertain of the love and security from the warmth of a proper relationship with mother and father is an unhappy child. For decades I have been favored and blessed with the acquaintance and friendship of a very fine Christian lady whose conduct and attitudes are exemplary. She had a long and successful career as a registered nurse, helping countless strangers, and her speech and manner with her fellow Christians have always set an admirably high standard. Truly, she is a bright light for the Savior. Still, many times through the years she has expressed to me, self-doubts of her own unworthiness as a Christian, even so far as to recall moments from her childhood and youth where she has lamented what troubles her as her own "deplorable" conduct. Am I really saved, am I truly a Christian she has lamented many times to me, probably just one person among countless others. Without any sense or to any degree usurping the authority of Christ Himself as Judge of the Universe, the answer is a ringing "yes" to her question of salvation. The pity is that too often in our usually righteous zeal to teach and preach and to personally strive for salvation unconsciously we in the Church have shifted the entirety of the responsibility of our own salvation to our own weak, easily burdened shoulders. In our strivings and the misplaced emphasis of Church teachings in the immediate past generations we have incorrectly shifted the "burden" of salvation to our own weak shoulders and have transformed Christ into a type of combination judge, referee and spiritual scorekeeper of each life. The amounts and depths of unhappiness and discontent that have been inculcated into the minds, spirits and lives of Christians who are loved as much as God loves His own Son is impossible to describe.

None of the above, though, is by any means a novelty, for the New Testament scriptures are quite open as to the widespread and deep nature of the struggles, often similar to ours, which bore heavily upon the early Christians. The endlessly circuitous argument of the source of salvation and the very ideas which spring from it are boldly noticeable in the New Testament. Does salvation come from faith, works or grace, or a combination in some manner of the three. Let us be as bold as are the scriptures. Man's salvation comes totally from the grace of God. It is not a question of discerning the right formula for a mixture of faith and works. As a bedrock foundation let us aver that salvation is totally a gift from God. It is not within man's capacity to direct his own footsteps. Quite simply, and to many quite bluntly, men and women can do nothing to save their souls, for salvation is entirely a gift from God. As the great evangelist Paul, as busy and work oriented as any person who ever lived, proclaimed:

> "Salvation is not of works, lest any man should boast."

The Christian does not make fresh claims daily upon God and is not building a type of spiritual invoice to later present for payment to the Almighty. Even if a Christian could do such a thing (and he cannot) the size of the invoice to God would be piteously, even laughably small compared to the invoice God submitted to us. Yet the blood of Christ, the most powerful expression of the grace of God, cleanses us daily from our sins. It is not our prayers, our good intentions, our good hearts or our good works. It is the shed of blood of Christ, and that alone which saves us and continues to hold our salvation secure.

Endlessly, even with a sort of mindfulness, the Word consistently refers to Christians as the children of God. Christ Himself told His disciples that to come to Him that follower must be as a "little child." No matter how old, how mature, how battle scarred by life, he or she may by the Christian wants the love and approval of mother and father, no matter the ages of the earthly components of this relationship. How pleasing, even heartwarming it is to a son or daughter, to be able to rest securely in the knowledge of parental love, approval and pride, even if the parents are no longer living. How terrible and unsettling is the opposite of living with a gnawing doubt, perhaps even a certainty, that those persons who brought you into the world and should love you with an unquenchable and unfathomable depth do not approve of you or even if their approval is continually vacillating. Sadly but truly this latter is the condition of many otherwise good, faithful Christians. It is the polar opposite of the security of the believer and the certainty of love and salvation. Daily this emotional frailty pilfers from untold numbers of Christians the peace that passes understanding, and they live in a realm of twilight, often afraid of the vengeful wrath of their own Savior. Do a father and mother in this life desire a beloved child to be continually whipsawed between certainty and doubt as to his love for the child? The answer to this question is splendidly and thoroughly given in the scriptures, most often directly from the Father and then from His Son.

The most common metaphor in the scriptures, practically to the point of ubiquity, which God employs to illustrate the relationship between Himself and His disciples is that of shepherd to sheep. Since sheep were so common in the Biblical lands, we should have no difficulty understanding why God continually employs such language. So many of the Old Book's key figures were shepherds, men such as Abel, Abraham, Moses and David, all of could, and in the case of David did, illustrate the Divine disciple relationship as that of shepherd to sheep. Both more vigorously and more touchingly did Jesus proclaim His relationship as that of shepherd to sheep. To emphasize forever such Divine self-identification He often referred to Himself as the Good Shepherd. It is instructive to the point of amazement that He purposely and lovingly so identified Himself. Just a mere days before His crucifixion Jesus looked upon the teeming crowds in Jerusalem and lamented that they were as "... sheep without a shepherd." Once and forever He proved the validity and depth of this love by giving Himself in a torturous death for all. The message of the Old and even more intensely the New Testaments is that His love is fiercely intense and that His grasp upon His own children is not easily loosened or broken. Broken it may become and the fall from His grace become a sad reality, but it does not easily occur. As recorded by His beloved apostle John He exclaimed:

> "And I gave them eternal life, and they shall never perish,

neither shall any man pluck them out of My hand."

The hands of the Savior are powerful and mighty and yet they are soft and gentle. So, is it impossible for a disciple to fall from God's grace, once saved and then lost? This question has been a hard, even harsh dividing line throughout centuries of Christendom, and yet remains. We aver, with the authority of the scriptures, that a Christian may "fall" from grace. In actuality, though, the "fall" is often a leap from the arms of the Savior, a leap that is consciously made.

Before we leave purely personal references and examples behind and confined to this Preface, our conclusion references a most famous parable of the Master, a parabolic story that is bursting with moral lessons which seem to germinate and multiply continually. In Christ's story, perhaps His most famous parable, a wealthy man had two sons, each of whom lived at home and still worked for him. The younger was anxious and excited to get going with his life and thus demanded from his father give him his portion of the inheritance. Promptly, he went into a far country, and in the famous words of Jesus there "... he wasted his substance in riotous living." Broke, despondent and filthy, now abandoned by his friends who were as easily repelled by his poverty as they had attracted by his money, the youth was reduced to feeding hogs, an unspeakable disgrace for a Jew. "He came to himself" and returned to his father, with a memorized set speech apologizing for his atrocious behavior. From a distance his father espied him, ran to his son and fell upon him with a cathartic flood of joyous tears. The youth began his confession, but was immediately halted by his father, who instead placed a luxurious robe about him, indicating his incalculable value to his father. The young man had never ceased being his father's son. In our titular language, yes, he really was a son still. With the facts and overwhelming emotions of such a revealing story of the love and grace of God we now proceed in an attempt to answer, "Am I Really a Christian?"

CHAPTER ONE

CHOICES

We cherish our choices. A person's life, presumably lived to a reasonabler number of years, is full of choices. Since we are carnal beings, our minds immediately move faster around the physical options that are presented to the average person. Our points will often be made in generalities, rather than to those exceptions to which any reader could easily raise. Every night we retire to rest and slumber, but the time in which our eyes close in repose is our choice. The time we arise the following morning, our daily routines and rituals, the nature and quantity of the food we consume is generally in our own purview. The chosen routine of life within the confines of our occupational choice defines so much of what each of our days consists. More importantly, for so much more, is the choice we make in the nature of our thinking and the attitudes which motivate conduct. Our essay could proceed boringly with an almost endless litany and miscellany of the choices that are presented to us with the rise of each morning's sun, yet the point is more quickly made. The physical realm in this world is the arena in which life is lived, but it is rightfully called temporal because it is temporary.

The physical, the mundane daily choices of life often direct the daily plodding of our footsteps, but the choices that really matter are far from temporal, time-bound and earth-bound but rather determine our future and eternity. The Father, the Creator of the Universe, from the very beginning had no desire to burden the pinnacle of His Creation, man, that piece of work made in the very image of God, with more choices than he could handle. God required only that Adam refrain from partaking of the fruit of one tree, that of the Knowledge of Good and Evil, but Adam and his wife Eve, the progenitors of all humanity, faced with the seemingly light burden of one choice only, that of obeying or disobeying God. In that time honored but well-worn cliché, the rest is history. The fall of man set the direction of humanity for the length of earthly tenure. Adam and Eve and their descendants were now to be (and so remain) flooded with an ocean of choices on how life was to be lived, and so it shall always remain. So easy it is, though, to neglect, overlook and even ignore that God was now faced with choices as to His own actions.

The prize of His creation, the human being, had failed miserably, and Biblical history itself confirms that God likely considered the destruction of His own creation. So repellant and repugnant had been the first man's sin that God easily could have chosen the extinction of His whole creation, or at a minimum man himself. Instead we now find and enjoy in part, some day to be wholly fulfilled the love and mercy reflected in the choices God made in overcoming man's fall and his seemingly ingrained sinfulness. To some extent speculating about God's choices in any given situation or moment is fraught with speculation. He is the Divine Creator and is not subject to the limitations which shadow mankind. God does, and did have, and so remains a Creator who has never ceased making choices.

God's great choice for humanity was its redemption and reconciliation to Him as matters had been in the beginning. Man was not destroyed, obliterated, cast into outer darkness, but God made the choice that He was to be redeemed, or more precisely, "repurchased" after his fall. Embodied in this is the entire story of the Bible, but let us indulge ourselves with the most beautiful exposition of God's choice, spoken thousands of years later by His own son:

> "For God so loved the world, that He gave His only begotten Son, that whosoever believeth in Him shall never perish, but have everlasting life."

God's choice was to love and to give, and to give the most valuable Creation in the universe and for the simple reason that "... He so loved the world." Death, which Satan had introduced into the world, would lose its dominion over man, and in those great words yet to be uttered, "... death, thou shalt die." Yet, the ultimate triumph was in the distant future, and in the meantime, much would be revealed about the true character of God. In modern legal litany the God of the Bible, the God of Creation and the one true God has never been arbitrary or capricious in his choices for His creation. They have all followed a pattern, and the desired culmination of that pattern is mankind's redemption ad salvation. Let us aver that if it must be delineated that all God's choices for humanity's salvation are either positive or negative, the Almighty has always chosen the positive, the best. Like a good parent choosing what is best for the child God made the choice, and yet still, to make things as easy as possible for His children.

When man fell, he fell long way, so deep that the means of his own extrication was absent. God would still be the Creator, the Master of the Universe, if He had looked upon this human, the homo sapiens, as degraded, despicable and not worthy of any more of His Divine time and attention. To our literal eternal blessing God made another choice, that selection of redeeming man to where he was initially meant to be. When the Almighty had finished His process of Creation, He had looked upon it and pronounced it "good." Not good as we mortals understand the term, but good in a spiritual Divine sense, of being perfect and complete. The apogee of His work was that being literally made "in the image of God." He was perfect, yet God still granted to Adam the choice of obedience or rebellion. Adam and Eve chose the latter, and thus the "Fall of Man." When man fell, he fell a long way into an abyss of sin and an ever-whirling maelstrom of Satanic devices and temptations. Only God could redeem his great creation and only through the greatest of all sacrifices, His own Son. Again, "For God so loved the world..." is more than a saying or a Biblical memory verse. The words from the lips of the Savior Himself are an everlasting pronouncement of God's intended relationship to man. He would be redeemed, but the redemption, the reconciliation and the perfection would be thousands of years in the revealing of its slow, but splendid realization. In the interim God, believe it or not, the most aggrieved parent in history, always meant matters and life to be as easy as possible. He knew that the Devil was always there to provide the perilous path of calamity and destruction.

Undoubtedly. In a physical sense humanity's existence in the early days of the world was rough, maybe rougher than what we moderns can delineate or even imagine. Man was forced to earn his living by the "sweat of his brow," and the lot of women, with the agonies and pangs of childbirth and lives of subjection was even worse.

Any person with even a nodding familiarity with the Old Testament is keenly aware that the millennia long path of God's disciples was not a rose bedecked lane. The Old Book speaks for itself, but let us remind ourselves that God had already made the choice to tend to and nurture His disciples, from physical hardship, famine, slavery, wars, rebellions, insurrections etc. He always furnished the choice for His Chosen, usually the Israelites, to follow Him. One of His greatest gifts to His people was the Law of Moses, mainly codified in the last four books of the Torah. The Law could be exacting and rigorous, but even to humanity, in its limited and blinkered wisdom, it was always fair, equitable and measurable. God had chosen for His people and as it was handed to them from Sinai a great blessing, an understandable and reasonable code by which His people could grasp the nature of their God. He could have chosen otherwise, but the Lord left it to the rulers of the world to select despotism and tyranny.

Sadly, the story of most of the Old Testament ranges between a horror story of the disciples' self-degradation and rejection of God to the calamities which rightfully befell them. God made choices, but all too often they were choices which were almost self-dictated by the behavior of His people. The northern bulk of the kingdom was gone forever in 722 B.C. when complete disregard led to the collapse of their nation. The southern kingdom of Judah retained a faith in God, albeit exercised too often with half-hearted devotion and continually sporadic. Still, God through immense temptations of an intensity only to be understood by God Himself, held true to the choice He had made, to save a "remnant" of Judah and thereby prepare the scene for the salvation of the world.

Regretfully, the Old Testament's chronicling of events ceases approximately four hundred years before the birth of Christ. Unsurprisingly, the history of the Jews remained turbulent and violent, primarily resulting from endless invasions of far more powerful foreign states but certainly in the mix was civil unrest which more than once erupted into civil war. This "between the testaments" period was a time when the Jews solidified themselves into a true nation. After countless centuries they finally began to identify as God's Chosen and took to themselves a pride in their ancestry, traditions and most of all the Law. Even then, though, the patience of God accrued no reward to the Lord, for His people became too enamored with the Law. Even that is not a full accommodation of their problem because as Christ would so powerfully demonstrate many Jews, especially their religious leaders, became slavish and even malicious in their own traditional interpretations of what they conceived the Law to be.

Nonetheless, in spite of all the difficulties the Jewish people created for themselves in their attitudes towards the Law God had chosen wisely. For much of their history the seed of Abraham had but a passing acquaintance with the Law as they chose to flatter and delight themselves in being more similar to the pagan Gentiles which surround their diminutive land. At times so little was it held in esteem that it had become in both a figurative and literal sense "lost" until workers in the seventh century B.C. reign of King Josiah, discovered a copy in the rubble of the old Temple. Josiah, Judah's greatest king, began a religious renaissance in Judah, proclaiming the windfall victory of finding the Law amidst the ruins. Eternal laudation and praise are accorded Josiah, but still the story of God's choices had not yet been told. God fashioned the Law perfectly for its purposes, but its purposes were incomplete and, in the end, unrewarding.

As the apostle Paul, as great a student and practitioner of the Law of Moses who ever lived later proclaimed the Law was "good" if a man used it lawfully. The Law of Moses was a choice God made for the Israelite people, who He determined would not be governed by the whims and caprices of kings, princes and warlords. Rather He gave His people a codification of His thinking so complete and exquisitely Western, societies and nations were built upon it. As perfectly constructed as was the Law of Moses it was not itself perfect. Its words and precepts could direct and rule the lives of observant men and women, yet it could not save them. Apparently, God made the choice that the Law would be regnant in the affairs of His people for over a millennium, but it was not an end to itself. In the Biblical phraseology "before the foundations of the world" the Father had chosen to save fallen humanity, and no statutory code, however great, could so accomplish His desire.

After the Jews return from Persian exile in the 400's B.C. the people themselves had choices to make, by far the most pertinent and consequential being whether they would, at last, reject or follow the Law. Unfortunately, as the generations tumbled one after another and Judah was beset with foreign invasion and internal dissension, the Jewish people chose to follow the Law. Unfortunately to the point of heartbreak it became not the pure Law God delivered to Moses but rather only the superstructure to which now adhered the peculiar secular, political and personal interpretation of the Law as advanced by the ruling political and intellectual oligarchy of the priesthood, the scribes, the Sadducees and perhaps most effectively the Pharisees. What these ruling cadres accomplished was to evolve the Law of Moses, itself in its purest terms strict but equitable and never unfair, into an unbearable burden which weighed with a constant heaviness on the backs of the people.

Again, as Paul said it was a burden and a "yoke of bondage" which they could not bear. Most importantly, though, its usage was limited and temporary, and it could never itself quench what is the innate thirst of mankind, eternal life and freedom from the curse of death.

This paragraph easily could begin with an exclamation that now God made His greatest and most important choice of all, when one day the angel Gabriel appeared to the young Mary of Nazareth and told her that she had been chosen to give birth to the Savior. The previous sentence is certainly true except for the inclusion of the word "now." God had made His choice to redeem mankind at a time which the two great apostles Peter and Paul both proclaimed was "... before the foundation of the world." God's choice of salvation for the pride of His creation was not a whimsical spur of the moment decision but instead the culmination of the foundational truth that "God so loved the world..." From this choice flow all God's blessings to His People.

The Lord made a choice that He has never required from a single mother or father, and that is to sacrifice a child, in His case the sacrifice of His only son. The horror and brutality of this choice was demonstrated at Calvary two thousand years ago only to make way for the glory and grandeur three days later when Christ arose from the grave. The Father's choices are ongoing and have been since Creation.

We have been speaking of the grandiosity of God's ceaseless choices, but what about the choices that "hit home" and fashion and affect our daily lives? Any Biblical review of God's history of His dealings and relationship's with the intended glory of His creation must provide due focus and consideration upon the Jewish people, who from the time of Abraham to the Advent of Christ were in fact and reality the Chosen of God. At the time of the advent of Jesus the Jews had after countless centuries shed their dalliance and even addiction to heathen idolatry. At least by the time of the Maccabean Revolt in the 160's B.C. they developed great pride in the singularity of their ethnicity as Jews, which, as has been noted, was fueled by an intense devotion to the Law of Moses. Their intensity and pride in the Law was of such fiery intensity that the heat of devotion began to warp their construction and interpretation of the very Law which they claimed to love. This subject alone can become a fertile seed bed for research, scholarship and writing, but from this we spare the reader. As always, with beauty and simplicity it is Jesus Himself who expressed with horror and disdain the choices the ruling religions elites had made in their interpretation of the Law:

> "Woe unto you, scribes and Pharisees, hypocrites! For you pay tithe of mint, anise and cummin, and have omitted the weightier matters of the law, judgment, mercy and faith: these ought you to have done, and not leave the other undone."

At the time of Christ's earthly ministry the Jewish religious and political complex had become honeycombed with avarice and corruption and had made the Law of Moses along with their peculiar and oppressive interpretations into a massive nationwide boulder which the Jews, no matter how sincere they might be, could not bear. Truly, it had become the "yoke of bondage" so aptly described in the New Testament. Generation after generation the choice of legalism, triviality, and minutia had been made, and with the advent of Christ He saw the people breaking under the burdens of religion, but not true religion. With His Son, God had made the decision to reveal His choice for humanity, and it may be synthesized into the beauty and simplicity of but one word. God's choice was, is and always shall be grace for His faithful, His disciples and His "Christians."

Never once has God wavered in His eternal commitment to grace, but the history of Christendom for two thousand years is at times a study of the varying interpretations His followers, real and putative have placed upon the word "grace." Even today the adherents of Jesus Christ, with varying levels of sincerity and commitment struggle with coming to terms with that ever so essential question, "Am I Really a Christian." Do I really follow Christ and ultimately was I saved, and do I remain saved from my sins? It is a plague upon Christendom, the Church and upon Christians individually, but it is certainly not new to our present age.

Early in the Church's history and especially as evidenced in the entirety of the New Testament two words and concepts began to dominate theological thought, not only of theologians and scholars but also of the ordinary Christian man and woman. The two words, today as ubiquitous as ever, are faith and works. Salvation from sin and death never did depend upon the factors so pronouncedly important by mankind in the Old Testament, and with the appearance, teachings and sacrifice of Christ such was confirmed. God had always made His choice that salvation depended not upon eternal indicia, all so important to humanity, such as the natural dichotomies of Jew/Gentile, male/female, rich/poor, all of which are part of the heavy baggage of each generation. Salvation came individually and came from one source only, the sacrificial blood of His Son, Jesus Christ. The Master Himself taught this for three years but after His departure left the specific enunciation to Peter, who pronounced on the Day of Pentecost only that the believer turn from sin, confess his/her belief and be baptized to acquire the title of

Christian (though such word had not yet been coined) to receive eternal life. On that day of the Church's founding over three thousand souls came to and obeyed Christ. Naturally, the question arose, an inquiry yet to be answered even to some Christians, of "what do I do now? I have the choice of Christ, but is that enough?"

At first and for several years to follow the demography of the early church provided some answers to that last question. Salvation came first to the Jews, but now many Jews began to accept and obey Christ. Certainly, they became Christians, our spiritual ancestors, but they remained Jews not just ethnically but Jews in spirit brought up in the truth and admonition of the Law. Most assuredly the very Church established by Christ Himself and been launched into a rocket-propelled start on Pentecost, and daily new converts were added to the saved. The came from so many locales, as the Book of Acts recounts by name a total of seventeen places from which they had come to Jerusalem for the annual celebration of Passover. In the flush of victory from the founding the Church was growing by the proverbial leaps and bounds. We are provided no numbers of its growth, for the New Testament itself offers only a paucity of numbers, the Word always concerning itself with the individual soul. Such was the Church's growth that early in its history Acts recounts that it had been remarked that the apostles "had turned the world upside down" with their preaching and teaching of a new doctrine, the person of Jesus Christ Himself. The Church, centered in Jerusalem at first, began to spread throughout Judea ad eventually the outer edges of the lands touched by the Jewish Diaspora. Many men and women had accepted and obeyed Christ, from numerous towns and regions, all ages, both sexes, etc., but for the first few years of the Church's existence all shared at least one similarity. All were Jews, the seed of Abraham and from their cradle reared in the fear and reverence of the guidance, strictures and the burdens of the Law of Moses. They had known nothing else, and it was only a natural outgrowth that their lives, set from infancy in the knowledge and observance of the Mosaical Law, would continue along the same path guided and directed by the signposts of demand and achievement known as the "works" of the Law. They had been, and rightfully so, proud to be Jews, just as doubtless now that they were (hopefully in the proper sense) "proud" to be Christians. The Law, its routines, liturgies, and structures had infiltrated these Jews, now Christians, and its precepts had guided them body and soul and penetrated to the very marrow of their bones. They acknowledged their Savior, Jesus Christ, the very Son of God, but while they were Christians, they were Jewish Christians. Something the Jews knew and had imbibed to the very rim of the cup is that they had to work for their salvation, a concept of no originality to them. The Law of Moses itself had been based upon the performance of so many works.

The times, though, were changing, and it was God Himself who generated the change, all in accord with His desires and thousands of years of prophecy. The Biblical worlds of Jew and Gentile were first joined where God dispatched the apostle Peter (a committed Jew if there ever was one) to speak to the Roman centurion Cornelius, a man of sterling character who sought to do right. Yet he was a Gentile, steeped in the cultural and religious darkness of paganism. He lived among the Jews, a man with great authority, yet he remained neither Jew nor Christian, but a Gentile. Daily Corneilus prayed to God, and his choice was to follow the Deity, but he needed guidance and such he received a visit from Peter and with the obedience of Cornelius, his family, and his servants, the Church truly became universal, both Jew and Gentile. Those terms, though, were more than just descriptions of ethnicity, but most importantly they were labels for two radically different world views. The Jews of the first century were steeped in laws and traditions, and vast numbers were sincere in their devotion to God. As for the Gentile world, in the words of the Master Himself, they had long dwelled in darkness.

Our narrative has noted that the New Testament rarely gives attention to numbers. Its text, though, the letters of the apostles, and history itself strongly suggests that the Church evolved with amazing velocity from exclusively where it remains even today, almost exclusively Gentile. The fusion of the two groups, even into the Body of Christ, was encumbered by a plurality of problems, but none more important than the clash of the relative lack of spiritual knowledge of the Gentile Christians with that of the previous exclusive claim of God's favor upon the Jews, who had long considered themselves (and rightfully so) God's Chosen. They lived by the Law and by their traditions of the Law, which the Gentiles had been engulfed by darkness. The Jewish Christians accepted the Gentile converts, albeit reluctantly, but not without conditions. Many, but not all the Jewish Christians had developed a hybrid faith, which was basically the old Judaism of the Law, overlaid with Christ as the Savior, but a Christ who had altered more into a latter-day Moses than the Son of God. These Jews would accept the Gentiles into the Church, however reluctantly, if the new Gentiles accepted the Law of Moses. In its simplest terms, become a Jew first, and then you can become a Christian, but only after evidencing your genuineness by following the Law of Moses. Although no serious Christian would ever deny that all life is a continuum of choices these early Judaizers had placed a number of obstacles in the paths of the willing Gentile convert that could be overcome only by a series of choices, some of which were never spoken of by Christ and most certainly never required by the Master. First, the Gentile seeking Christ and salvation had to turn from the darkness and degradation of the Gentile world. Bravo! we exclaim for such a repentance is required of any Christian. The repentances taught and offered (still) by Christ was to turn from sin to the embrace and euphoria of being in the flock of the Savior Himself, or in a term of one word to be a Christian, or a "little Christ." Not so said the Judaizers but really before coming to Christ, no matter how sincere, eager and repentant the Gentile sinner might be he had to pass through a type of hybrid Jew's-Christian life experience and first become a Gentile version of a Jew. Should any wiling Gentile ask our eponymous question of "Am I Really a Christian?" the Judaizers' response would be a resounding "no" or perhaps more hopefully "not yet." So wedded to the Law of Moses and its customs, traditions and the Jewish way of life that even many early Jewish Christians could not conceive of a world where anyone but a Jew, or a proselyte Jew from the Gentile world, could be acceptable to God.

The Judaizers effectively and even sternly preached to the Gentile to come to Christ yes, but come to Moses first. These Jewish Christians seemed to accept only with a decided reluctance that a Gentile could ever be acceptable to God, but ... so be it. If this was God's desire their ordination was that the Gentile must first pass through and always continue a scrupulous keeping of the Law of Moses. They could not even begin to be considered "real Christians" until they made the choice to come to Christ through a labyrinth of laws, customs and traditions. To these Jews, though they be followers of Christ themselves, in their presumed spiritual possession was a commission to require all men and women to be as near replicas of themselves, even though they were ever to be hindered by their

Gentile ancestry. The Gentile convert in their view was not really a Christian until he was first a Jew

Being a Jew, a descendant of the seed of the great patriarch Abraham meant rigid observance of law, periodic sacrifices, hold days, obeying the dictates of the religious oligarchy, the various Sadducees, priests, Pharisees and scribes who were in fact continually distorting the Law according to their views and adding burdens on the backs of the people, or as Jesus said a "yoke of bondage" which they could not bear. While it was not actual bondage or human slavery it was a spiritual and life-style strait jacket which Christ Himself said could not be borne without collapse. Most specifically it meant the strictures of the Law, and it meant works whereby their souls might be saved. But was this the choice which God and his only Son had made? Did and do men and women have to "earn" their eternal salvation by the sweat of their brows? Succinctly stated, the answer is an eternally thunderous "no," for if salvation is by law and works Christ's death was in vain and of no account.

Jesus Christ had come to earth and in the purest, most complete fashion possible fulfilled thousands of years of prophecy, defeated Satan and his weaponry of death and opened the gates of Heaven to all. Neither sin nor Satan died, but their great, grinding oppression had been lifted from the backs of humanity. With the path of Light now open to mankind what did he seek to do? Sadly, it was not just the teachers of Judaism but many in the two millennia since, some from nefarious motives and others well-meaning have sought to place stumbling blocks, boulders and mountains of burdens between the Son of God and His flock.

Unfortunately, the Jewish people in large measure rejected Christ and abandoned Christianity long ago. From the New Testament and the clear record of history by the conclusion of the Biblical era the Church was becoming increasingly the province of Gentiles; however, while they may belong to antiquity the ideas and doctrines of the Judaizers have not vanished. Christians of Gentile heritage have been equally masterful in finding untold and unauthorized burdens to place upon the backs of Christian disciples. An excellent, made to order scene, to study and discuss the question of just who may consider himself or herself not only a Christian, but a faithful Christian has been provided by one of the earliest New Testament books, the epistle of the apostle Paul to the Galatians. Here, as a supplement to Christ's teachings may we find the answer to the question "Am I Really a Christian."

CHAPTER TWO

FLESH AND SPIRIT

History at many junctures is an oddity in that certain events, clashes, controversies and even the lives of men and women do not necessarily arise or occur in the places that seem logical, at least to the modern mind. Galatia was a region in north central Asia Minor (basically modern-day Turkey) mostly and at times exclusively removed from the pageantry of the Old Testament story. Geographically, it was perhaps a thousand miles from what became the greatest and most powerful city of antiquity Rome. In fact, Galatia was so far removed from the Italian metropolis that it was not annexed and made a Roman province until 25 B.C., somewhat late in the great expansionist period of the Empire.

Historically and religiously Galatia had little contact with Israel and Judah and is not even mentioned in the Old Testament. By the first century A.D. its population did include a representative number of Jews who had settled there in the great Diaspora of the Jewish people. They remained the Chosen of God but evidently found their place and prospered in this new world of Galatia, a region whose basic populous was far removed from the Jews by history, culture, physical appearance and most of all by religion. It is for present examination the nature and background of the "Galatians."

Ethnically, the Galatians were unlike almost all people whose stories compose both testaments of the Bible. Most of the Old Testament is the story of the Hebrew people, the nation's of Israel and Judah, or in shortened parlance "the Jews." Similarly, the New Testament's first four Books, the gospels, and much of its remaining pages still have Jewish persons in prominence. The new book, though, began to intersperse with the Jews increasing numbers of Greeks and Italians from the classical European civilizations. Overall (for what it is worth) the Holy Bible focuses upon the Mediterranean people and their culture. The majority of its subjects, most prominently by far, the Jews are Semitic. But now we turn our eyes to this remote region on the eastern edge of the Roman Empire and with curiosity inquire "who were the Galatians and where did they come from?" In the third century before Christ a very large group of people who lived throughout central and northern Europe, the Celts, began vast migrations to other lands. Many went westward to the British Isles and became the ancestors of the Scots, the Irish and the Welsh. A huge group, the Gauls, made the journey to that large area which eventually became France and while they founded not a nation in the modern sense, were so powerful that they were not subdued until the armies of Julius Caesar himself forced their capitulation in the 50's B.C.

Another branch of the Gauls went not west but south and east and settled into Galatia, the name of which is obviously extracted from "Gaul." These Celts, including the Galatians, bore certain physical dissimilarities to other Biblical ethnicities. Whereas in the main (though by no means exclusively) the latter usually bore a somewhat darker, basically olive complexion, dark hair and brown eyes, while most of the Gaulish people, including the Galatians were fair with lighter, even blonde hair, and quite commonly blue-eyed. They Stood out, and yes "standing out" is usually noticed in all societies by they ancient or modern. Although their panoply of gods and goddesses was different from those of the Greeks and Romans the Galatians were heathen to the core.

The Galatians remained people "without light" in the words of the Savior Himself, until Paul and his companions came there circa 50 A.D. and were very successful in establishing new churches. How many and what was the number of their adherents we know not, but Paul's expedition was a resounding success. Paul, the Divinely appointed apostle to the Gentiles, had fabulous success, but it was not limited. Many Jews, a people who became increasingly resistant and intransigent in opposition to Christianity, and thus many churches were established throughout Galatia. It remained an odd mixture of people, though, a group that for generations had been steeped in the Law of Moses now mingling with a "strange" Gentile people who had been steeped in another brew, the concoction of paganism with its multiplicity of deities, violence, adultery, and dishonesty. It was a grouping, soon to be experienced in many places, that was bound to be combustible with more fire than light.

Presumably the Galatian Jews were a part of the commonality of all humanity and bore some resentment to the Gentiles' presence at the table. The Galatian idea of the Deity, to the extent that they had them, was that of an ever-increasing assemblage of pagan beings, whose mythical morality could be even worse than humans. The Jewish concept of God, and the intensity and accuracy of feeling depended upon the individual Jew was a God who ordained the Ten Commandments at the head of a complex, complete and beautifully written Law of Moses. Here was the character of God, a Creator who loved but was demanding, almost to a problematic and to some an impossible degree. He required strict obedience to a moral code which obliged its adherents to a lifetime of strict obedience to the Father and proper treatment and respect to one's neighbors. Moral purity, honesty and integrity permeated every syllable of the Law's tenets. Most definitely this was not the moral ground from which sprang the Gentiles of Galatia wo had followed Christ. The New Testament writers, most prominently Paul, were not coy and were unsparing of the Gentile lifestyle from whence these new Christians came. Their lives had been guided not by morality but an unwritten moral code which extolled slavery, marital infidelity, the grossest and most perverse forms of sexual immorality, deception, and in general self-centered and self-willed conduct. The Galatians' moral education had been the polar opposite of the Jews. Now, though, here they were, 'brothers and sisters in Christ" with the same Savior, the same path to heaven and the same morality of righteousness. Still in so many ways, including ways that are perhaps unimaginable to us now the two groups, Jew and Galatian, were so starkly different. The Jewish Christians, most brought up in the faith from their mother's womb and the Galatian Christian, a Gentile and besides a Gentile only a few generations removed from the barbarous ancestral homelands of central Europe. All had obeyed Christ, both Jew and Galatian, with all having been baptized into the faith, but an enormous question mark was fastened by the Jews upon their new Galatian brothers and sisters. Were these people, asked many of the Jews, really Christians? Paul's letter to the Galatians examined this question thoroughly. The Jews' answer to it by declaration and conduct was "not yet."

The Jews' answer to the above question, though, was not as brutally disregarding, callous and even haughty and self-righteous as it may sound. The answer of the Jewish Christians to the question did not indicate that the Jews intended to cast these would be pseudo-Christian Galatians back into the world. With sincerity many Jewish Christians were willing to accept and bestow fellowship upon the Gentiles upon one condition, a condition of enormous ethnic assimilation and equally enormous complications. The Jewish Christians would accept the Galatian Gentiles into the flock if first they became Jews. Certainly the Jews, a people of generally surpassing intelligence knew that no Gentile could change the nationality and ethnicity of his genetic heritage and birth. If though they followed the guideposts of the Law, including circumcision and observed the Law and its traditions the Jews would "embrace," them, however unwillingly lingered the contrary feelings of their hearts.

The inspiration of the brilliant apostle Paul devotes most of his Galatian letter to the dismantling of the Jews' arguments and requirements for the Gentiles. With so much deeply analytical yet eternally quotable language Paul demonstrates the fallacy of anyone, be they Gentile or Jew, following the Law of Moses, which was now dead, but still not absent from the hearts and minds of so many Jews, including many who had accepted Christ. Some few we will note, but hopefully not to the point of tedium. It was, however, in another letter which Paul authored, that to the church in Colossi, where the fate of the Law of Moses was declared. There, in an outburst of oration, beautiful in its simplicity Paul exclaimed:

> "(Christ), blotting out the handwriting of ordinances that was against us, which was contrary to us, and took it out of the way, nailing it to the cross."

The Law of Moses met its death on Calvary when the blood of Jesus Christ was shed for the world's atonement and forgiveness. It had been God's plan for over a millennium when it was given to Moses on Mount Sinai, but it was a dead letter. God's approval, his majesty and His indwelling with the disciple begins when, again in the apostle's words a person is "... buried with Him in baptism" and become one with Him. The one undeniable and essential element is answering the question of this book's title is whether the inquirer is one with Christ.

To the contrary the world, its religions and as we have seen even Christians themselves often feel duty bound and commissioned to add further elements to the requirements of being a "real" Christian. Did its Founder, Christ, leave the world in a state of permanent confusion as to the identity of His followers. What is more important to us and dare we say to Christ is whether His own followers, the Christians, have security in our identity and in salvation itself? Ere our narrative proceeds with an attempted answer(s) to these questions, the intentions, the work and the effects of the Judaizing teachers among the Galatians is to be considered.

The Galatian population was a people ripe for teaching, for instruction, for guidance but unfortunately also for errors. Not only from paganism did they come but from a particularly virulent form of it. These Galatians, now often city dwellers on the Anatolian Plateau of ancient Asra Minor, were only recently removed not just from heathen practices, but those in their most primitive forms. From the woodlands of central and eastern Europe and the plains of the north had they immigrated. Their religion had been the typical paganistic worship of multiple deities, but it also included a bountiful supply of gods and goddesses, perhaps even more despicable than those of the more cultured Greeks and Romans. This was the religious backdrop of these Galatians, but like most heathen religion it did not cultivate and foster a sense or spirit of high morality. They had their attributes did these Galatians. They are historically reputed to be a strong, tough, independent people, qualities that were essential to even survive the rigors and brutalities of ancient times. Such, though, did not prove fertile for the rise of finer qualities. In the mass the Galatians had a reputation for drunkenness, reveling, all the usual manners and modes of sexual immorality and profligacy which so besmirched the character of the Gentile world. While they were intellectually curious, perhaps even in matters of religion, they, as the eponymously titled epistle of Paul shows, were a fickle people, easily changeable in belief and practice and were ripe for errancy led by new ideas and new teachers, of which they were fond. In too many cases these new and now Christian Galatians were sumptuously prime targets for the Judaizing teachers, radically different than the Gentiles in culture, traditions, physical appearance but most especially in knowledge of God. Still, both groups, Jews and Galatians, had possessed the knowledge, determination and courage to follow a new light, the true "Light of the World," Jesus Christ. The knowledge gap between Jew and Gentile, though, was enormous, and many of these new Jewish Christians showed no hesitancy in taking advantage.

Whether the words ever passed their lips or even the idea their thinking, the Jewish Christians of Galatia, henceforth the "Judaizers" had drilled into the minds and the hearts of the new Galatian contends that titular and terribly ominous question "... am I really a Christian." The Judaizers with a resounding and oppressive adamancy answered the question "no, but you can become a Christian." To these apostatizing and legalistic Jews the path to Christ was open to the Galatians and any other Gentiles, but first they had to pass one monumental requirement. To the

Judaizers to be a true Christian one, no matter the background, religious cachet, or ethnicity, no matter his or her obedience to the simple commands of Christ as taught by His apostles, he/she first had become a "Jew" and follow the decrees of the Law of Moses.

The churches of Galatia founded by Paul and companions circa 50 A.D. had gotten off to a sensational start. Still, the combustibility of the Galatian church's compilation was intensively explosive. Perhaps it is to the Judaizing teachers the dubious honor is to be accorded of being the first proponents of the fallacy, sometimes sincerely presented but more often with a certain malice aforethought that a man or woman must do something or be somebody to be saved and considered a faithful Christian, a disciple of Christ and a member of his flock. To be a real Christian, satisfactory to its founder Christ, a person must be something more than, well, a Christian. It was a pernicious heresy then and two thousand years hence the present religious world of Christianity, i.e. Christendom, is no less afflicted with this virus.

The word "diversity" is a shibboleth in our presumably advanced modern age, a code word for a goal of which they desire (or at least think they deserve), a society that is a kaleidoscopic rainbow of many hires, many cultures and many beliefs living together in some sort of pantheistic or even extra-worldly harmony. The stark fact of the nature of the homo sapiens creature is that we almost instinctively are more comfortable with those who are most similar to us, be it language, race, ethnicity, and certain religious beliefs. The Jews for centuries had been specifically chosen by God to carry the human lineage that would give birth and reality to a Savior, Christ. They were special, felt special and reveled in being special. Now they were confronted with the stark honor of being bidden to accept the Gentiles as brothers and sisters, or in other terms to be "... one in Christ."

The Judaizers would accept, albeit with muted enthusiasm these strange Galatians as brothers, but only following a lengthy probationary period whereby they would be required to prove their newfound spiritual worthiness to the Jews. It would commence with the rite of circumcision, a symbol which God ordained through Moses as a signifying factor separating His then chosen people, the Jews, from the world. The faithful Jews had practiced it and still placed an essentiality upon it, and now the ritual would be required of the Gentiles. Yet the Christian teaching was that "neither circumcision nor uncircumcision availeth anything" but rather the answer of a good conscience towards God. Had the Judaizers stopped with this doctrine perhaps the eccentricity and quirkiness of their beliefs could have been managed. Unfortunately, this was the starting, not the stopping point. Christ and His apostles, most particularly Paul, at one time the most committed, even fanatical Jew ever, remarked that if one begins to keep a portion of the Law he became a debtor to the entirety of the Law. With circumcision came the keeping of the Sabbath and its multitudinous constrictions on living, feast and holy days, obedience to the priestly caste and the ever-increasing burdens the religions oligarchy could place upon them. The Judaizers adamantly and with ringing bells proclaimed to the new Gentile Christians that "No, you are not really a Christian." Or at least not until you fall in line with our ordained program of legalism and works. While Christ may have proclaimed that He had come to remove the "yoke of bondage" which was the Law and to set mankind free from sin, the Judaizing teachers proclaimed, "not so fast," for they had their own program, detailed, specific, rigid and demanding, which had to be scrupulously followed before any could even begin to consider himself or herself "really a Christian." Sadly, even dreadfully, the Judaizing teachers of Galatia would not be an isolated phenomenon but rather the lead in a philosophical and religious parade that remains current even today.

To a Christian little or nothing is sadder than to review the history of Christ's church and see that almost from the inception many teachers, would be authorities and a miscellany of religious activists that constantly sought to define, redefine and then define some more what it really means to be a Christian, and these lapses into a type of dictatorial apostasy remain, and likely always will, unabated. To many not even the throne of Christ has remained inviolate. For a moment let us raise our gaze from first century Galatia to the ensuing centuries' history of the Church and its gradual apostasy. The apostasy has been and remains so pronounced that the very cornerstone of the Church's foundation. Jesus Christ Himself has been augmented and supplanted by a Roman papacy whose head claims to set on a presumed earthly throne of Christ with the right to issue edicts and decrees possessing the Divine infallibility that is vouchsafed only in God. But the Roman Catholic papacy and hierarchy, most conspicuous as it may be, is not the disease, but only a highly visible manifestations of the problem. Great corrective measures and doctrines were boldly and courageously revived in the fifteenth and sixteenth centuries by reformers such as Martin Luther, John Calvin and countless others, who tried, albeit with inconsistency, to redirect the path of Christendom back to the light of scripture. Their teachings helped free many from the artificiality of restrictions, liturgy and manmade commandments which has surpassed even the tedious entrapment of the ancient scribes and Pharisees. They too were men, though, and too often they substituted their own thoughts and created concepts of religious belief and practice that themselves were athwart the Word of God. In recent centuries many have hungered for the simplicity of truth and the restoration of the original Church established by Christ in the first century.

Almost all groups which consider themselves Christian and a part if not the whole of Christendom are over organized, usually overstaffed and overdemanding of their members in matters that are at best incidental to Christianity and at worst detrimental. We Christians and our churches and their accompanying "organizations" have a marked tendency to slowly sidle into that territory for which Jesus pronounced the harshest condemnation upon the scribes and Pharisees:

> "For they bind heavy burdens and grievous to be borne, and lay them on men's shoulders; but they themselves will not move them with one of their fingers."

Doubtless the scribes and Pharisees and the later Judaizing teachers in Galatia started with at least a modicum of good intentions, but all were transforming the Church, a blood bought institution into something which Christ, its founder, never desired. Just as likely most of the early churchmen in the first generations of the Church of Christ believed with great sincerity, they were doing the Lord's work when they, slowly at first, began to give greater weight to structure, organization and position then to the simple but immeasurably deep and simple moral precepts of Jesus of Nazareth. In the Church's early history "power" centers began to develop. The simplicity of organization which Christ taught, and His apostles amplified began to slowly make room for more officials, more prelates, ladders and organizational charts of responsibility and certainly power. One man, be he deemed elder, presbyter, or bishop began to assert authority over others, even churches with which he was personally unacquainted, and even that was not enough. Bishops became subordinate to archbishops and the latter to cardinals and ultimately to the Roman papacy. Orders, directives, and pronouncements came from church officialdom rather than the simple moral teachings of the New Testament. Although this may be striking to many as a diatribe against the Roman Catholic Church, it is hoped that the point is not so truncated. All large bodies, including churches in whatever structure, be it Catholic, Orthodox, Protestant, or other began to lapse into a quagmire of structure and power centers. From these waters spring many problems, and easily a casualty to such apostasy in the individual Christian. In such a religious world, be it ruled by Judaizing teachers, Catholic priests or Protestant clergy the simple individual Christian may feel himself shrinking in importance to where he or she feels that nothing remains other than to be a cog in a religious machine of laws, rules and regulations fashioned by his church "superiors." Maybe it was in the Galatia of the 50's A.D. wherein this thinking and co-opting of Christianity began, but it flourishes in today's modern Christendom. The individual Christian then rightly asks "am I really a Christian" or just a small part, a gear, in a church machine.

Should we attempt to answer this last question ourselves, relying upon our own senses, our own presumably keen spiritual eyesight and follow it wherever such a road leads. Without attributing to any person "Satanic" or "devilish" purposes let us remember the first Edenic temptation of the serpent:

> "Ye shall not surely die.
> But God doth know that in the day ye eat thereof,
> there your eyes shall be opened, and ye shall be
> as gods, knowing good and evil."

Man's reliance on his own eyesight has long and ever shall it continue lasts only until his death. It is not only a poor guide, but a valueless one. The beautiful simplicity of the truth as spoken by Christ and His inspired apostles is discernible. Our God, the quintessence of a loving Father could never be so cruel as to intent His children, the disciples and flock of His Son, the Good Shepherd to live in a state of uncertainty, doubt and even fear. The answers are, of course, from the fount of all truth, the Christian's Shepherd and the Founder of His Church who lit the path of understanding for the answer to this question while delivering the Sermon on the Mount:

> "You shall know them by their fruits."

Like all men and women, the Christian or the worldly, by their fruits, or by the conduct of their lives we are known. It is in the letter of Galatians where the apostle specifically enumerated those fruits, but only after listing the following "works of the flesh" for a stark contrast:

> "Now the works of the flesh are manifest, which are these, adultery, fornication, uncleanness, lasciviousness, idolatry, witchcraft, hatred, variance, emulations, wrath, strife, desertions, heresies, envyings, murders, drunkenness, revellings and such like."

The sludge and sin of this sewer is then starkly delineated by the "... fruit of the Spirit", which is:

> "Love, joy, peace, longsuffering, gentleness, goodness, faith,
> Meekness, temperance, against such there is no law."

The Bible is not loath to provide contrasting examples of these qualities, to which we now turn our gaze.

CHAPTER THREE

LOVE, MARRIAGE AND ADULTERY

The first stanza of an old, a very old, standard American song, as most famously lyricized by none other than Frank Sinatra read:

> "Love and marriage, love and marriage go together like a horse and carriage,
> This, I tell 'ya brother, You can't have one without the other."

A few bars later he croons "... it's an institute you can't disparage." Oh really. As these few lines from a dated song from a long bygone cultural world are affixed, we realize the datedness, perhaps even the antiquity, of their sentiments. Except in certain tourist locales on the Pennsylvania Dutch Amish country "horse and carriage" is a quaint reference to a distant past quite unlikely to ever return. So be it, as time, mechanical and technological progress no longer just marches on but instead hurtles itself forward at an ever-dizzying rate. Of course the sentiments almost reek of a type of cultural formaldehyde with the line "... You can't have one without the other." Forces of modernity, sophistication and pseudo sophistication have accomplished marvels in making and at least in the eyes of many proving that such is not the case.

Be comforted by the promise that the reader will be spared a sojourn into the sunbaked rocks and sands of the desert of statistics to prove this assertion. While marriage certainly is extant, and even flourishing, among vast numbers of persons, it has fallen upon very hard times in the matter of culture and those mysterious forces which so shape popular belief. Within the life's memory of the older generation (including the author) is the knowledge of a time when marriage was the cornerstone of the structure of building blocks which was at the base of society, at least that of Western culture and primarily the United States. The majority of the population married young, quite young, and in so many instances too young. Yet marriage was the base of family, of community, of the nation and was believed strongly to be the vehicle by which men and women expressed their deepest emotions, feelings and desires. Most, certainly not all, the societal sector agreed on its vitality and indispensability to a strong community. Certainly, we have no desire to gild the picture with too much gold since even the strongest and most moral societies have always contained a marked plethora of bad, unhealthy and even hateful marriages, and unfortunately so shall it always be.

Still, as hard as it may be for newer generations to accept marriage was once the recipient of a broad consensus of support. Amazingly, be they Protestant, Catholic, Jewish or otherwise the consensus, even the enthusiasm, for marriage was quite broad and encompassed individuals of starkly different religious beliefs, ethnicities and various economic and cultural strata in society. Even such doubtful and admittedly dubious cultural outposts as the entertainment industry gave lip service to the good of marriage. Motion pictures, even early television and popular music as evidenced by Mr. Sinatra's song extolled its wonders and virtues. Certainly as with all virtuous desires elements of hypocrisy were attached, as witnessed Sinatra, a man world renown for philandering and multiple marriages.

The collapse of the preponderant popular marital ideal likely began with the ideas long inseminated in society but not truly bursting forth until the late 1960's and especially the 1970's. In popular cultural outlets marriage is often seen as either an antiquated institution clung to by religious "fanatics" who are themselves trapped in a loveless partnership. Or perhaps it is presented quite realistically as a temporary arrangement, a way station in life, until a better opportunity comes along. For the majority, the ideal of long-term marriage is no longer one of the great goals of life to be fulfilled. It is not seen as a unique relationship of companionship, partnership, intimacy, even eroticism but rather an old clunking relic of a benighted past. In such an accepted view we easily envision a luxuriating Satan. Of a certainty such a view of marriage is not new or novel in any sense and did not suddenly erupt upon the scene in the late twentieth and early twenty-first centuries. In whatever time, culture, society, financial state or otherwise doubtless an almost infinite number of marriages have been unhappy, miserable, even violent and brutal. They become partnerships in misery and calumny, and the spirit of Satan dwells within them.

Yet what of the other view, the original ordained view of God as the proper nature of a marriage. The Creator started with the basics and a basic purpose:

> "Therefore shall a man leave his father and mother, and shall cleave and they shall be one flesh."

The world's history from its earliest stages was revealing of man's desire to refashion the Divine Institution in different variations. Most races, ethnicities and cultures have honored marriage in some fashion from the outset. The manifestations of this "honor" have varied from slight difference to radical distinction from the original Edenic ideal of "one man, one woman, for life." The consummation of desire and erotic love more often than not has rarely paused for the formality of marriage in most cultures, most places and for most of the time.

The Old Testament, so often wildly misrepresented as the story of a tyrannical, despotic God who struck people, even His chosen, dead for the slightest infraction, in reality tells the story over several millennia of a God with literally Divine patience with the weaknesses of His creation. Polygamy, so common and almost endemic to heathen societies, began to flourish even among the chosen Israelites, especially its upper and most definitely its monarchial ranges. Kings David and Solomon and so many others were hardly paragons of marital virtue and seemed to take almost whimsically at times any desirable female who sparked his cravings. Even the great patriarch Jacob had two wives plus other young women to sate his desires. The marital and sexual profligacy of most of the Gentile people is almost impossible to meaningfully convey. Even the most advanced of them, the Romans, made a mockery of marital fidelity for much of modern society. The Romans were, in theory at least, essentially monogamous, but marital bonds could be broken at the whim of the husband. The blue-blooded aristocrats, i.e. the patricians, were notably representative of this conduct.

Anyone who has been a student of Roman history is well aware of the dizzying speed with which the Roman upper crust, would marry, divorce and remarry with what seems to the initial glance senseless abandon but often were cold calculations made to advance a senator's or even a Caesar's career. The marital history of many of antiquity's most famous persons, both Gentile and shamefully even Jew, is a confusing litany of additional or substitute spouses, often with the reasons being not even barely disguised political machinations. The Romans, who with self-congratulations, make themselves awash in their own self-praise for the ancient Gentilic version of "family values." Undoubtedly there existed and even flourished fine Roman families, but this is the culture, the people and the legal system that introduced and popularized the concepts of divorce at will and what became known in modernity as "no-fault" divorce.

The Jews, the chosen themselves, even as the late centuries B.C. rolled forward with their becoming more stringent and serious in the commitment to the Law could not quite see marriage in its proper state. Unsurprisingly it was the Master Himself, Jesus Christ, in His brief earthly ministry, who reminded all of His Father's original intentions for marriage:

> "Moses because of the hardness of your hearts suffered (allowed) you to put away your wives: but from the beginning it was not so."

This bespeaks a sad truth, and certainly of all persons the Son of Man knew this. With so many persons, past, present, and future, there is a type of immoral centrifugal force that seems to spin and launch them away from marital vows and bonds. Now, though, with the coming of Christ and His founding of Christianity God's original desire for the union of man and women for life was made manifest not from prophets, priests, or even apostles but from the voice of the Savior Himself. Still, they fall on so many deaf ears and so many turn even love and marriage, God's first Divinely created institution into an abyss of immoral heartache and calamity.

But before the gloom of moral darkness totally engulfs this chapter let us look at two polar opposite marriages of persons of basically contemporary age. One illustrates the "works of the flesh" within marriage and the other offers for all eternity a particularly poignant example of marital commitment and love as a "fruit of the Spirit." Two marriages, and yes both between a man and a woman, yet our examples will be illustrative of the wretchedly immoral grandeur of the man even before marriage. The respective similarities of their spousal partners certainly will not go unnoticed, but the focus will be upon two very important persons in first century Judea, doubtless each personally unknown to the other. Their names are Herodias and Joseph.

Herodias

For centuries the Herod family had loomed over Judean skies as a Stygian black bird of prey to feed off the wounded nation over which they exercise great influence and control, though always under the suzerainty of the Romans, the ultimate earthly power in the west. The four gospels and into the book of Acts are filled with the evils of the Herod family, and all have been the backdrop for study of insidious, nefarious evil which was an affront to God. It began with King Herod the Great, the original would-be murderer of the infant Messiah, through his son Herod Antipas, Herod Antipas I, a man whose appetite for fame and power was resistant to satisfaction and to a lesser extent, the very last of the Herod of notoriety, King Herod Agrippa II. Their stories have been told and analyzed repeatedly for two millennia, but it is not them upon which we focus our gaze but rather one woman with a confusingly ubiquitous name of Herodias. None of our narrative seeks to absolve any of the Herod men of their sins but for now we calibrate the historical microscope to focus and examine the character of an evil woman.

Herod Antipas, a man perhaps in his mid-forties at the time of our story, ruled over Galilee and Perea, the very territories in which John the Baptist and his cousin Jesus of Nazareth concentrated their ministries. Antipas had been successful in wresting these territories from the control of his older brother Archelaus, but his political ambitions were not yet sated. In the late 20's A.D. he went to Rome to visit his half-brother Herod Philip. Philip was married to a woman named (in all confusion) Herodias, a lady with a contemporary and historical reputation of beauty. Antipas swooned at the sight and the personality of Herodias, and perhaps each of this pair saw the other as a great aid in boosting them up the political ladder. After much intrigue, better described elsewhere, Herodias was divorced from Philip and married Antipas. This itself was a grossly outrageous violation of the Law of Moses, a code to which the Herod's, part-Jews, claimed some allegiance, especially when it was convenient.

After their apparently wildly successful venture in Rome the newlywed couple of Herod Antipas and Herodias returned to Perea. There in his home base Antipas planned a great feast, banquet and extravaganza to which the local high society would all be attendees. All was not calm on the home front though. A new religious rabbi, a strange man of a wild character, John the Baptist, had begun to proclaim with a thundering vociferousness that this was the most blatant form of adultery, inasmuch as the Law had expressly forbade a man to marry his brother's wife, made even worse by the fact that the brother of Antipas, Philip, was still living. Antipas seemingly was able to withstand the moral teachings of John the Baptist, but not so for Herodias. At her insistence, Herod Antipas, had John incarcerated in a prison. Antipas was in no way repulsed by John the Baptist and in fact enjoyed a continuing rapport with him, constantly speaking and listening with great interest to his teachings. Not so, however, with Herodias.

Herodias hated John the Baptist, and the fullness of the reasons therefor has always been speculative. Certainly, she was outraged that this scruffy wild man, the prophet of a new religion of which she and her social set no doubt made an object of jest and ridicule, would have the temerity to call her, the veritable "first lady" of the land an adulterer. Still she was canny enough to know that the Jews took religion very seriously and her worries that John's blunt denunciation would prove incendiary to the public must have lurked in her mind. For all this, though, likely she hated John the Baptist with such fury and deadly intensity because evil hates good. The most potent manifest of this is the hatred that Satan bears God, and ever shall it be.

Herodias had marked John the Baptist for death, and she was acquiring the weaponry for the necessary coup de' grace. Herodias provided the viperous venom, Antipas the forum and occasion and a young girl named Salome the deadly weapon of sensual allure. It remains one of the most famous scenes not only in Biblical history but all history. The moment has been depicted in the cinema, in books, art, and all forms of communication, including its recounting by the present author. The structure of the story will not be delineated in detail again but suffice it for our present purposes it was stark a scene of "the works of the flesh" which could be described. Antipas was assembled with all the great men, political, military, business, perhaps a cleric or two to celebrate his royal birthday. As the evening progressed the alcohol flowed freely, the bawdiness of Herod and his guests was reaching a fevered pitch when the apogee of the evening's entertainment was attained. A luscious, nubile young woman named Salome would dance for them. And dance she did in one of history's most celebrated performances, described as anything from a well performed ancient Eastern dance to little else but a salacious striptease. Whatever its artistic quality it worked with Herod Antipas. Salome, both Herod's stepdaughter and his niece, by blood and not marriage captivated Antipas with her youthful enticements and by the dance's end his hormones were floating in a sea of alcohol. Name your price, Herod told his delightful nymph Salome, and anything up to half my kingdom is yours for the asking. Salome, so young, was unaccustomed to responding to such a request, so naturally she consulted her mother Herodias, who had no trouble or hesitation in offering her daughter a strongly suggested reply:

> "Give me the head of John the Baptist in a charger."

Two thousand years hence it retains an impact and is literally one of the most famous pronouncements in human history. Ruefully, upon hearing the request Antipas, one of history's most pathetic men, acceded to it, and the Christ proclaimed greatest of all prophets met his death. Herod Antipas possessed in full measure that great trifecta of qualities that have and so continue to bring destruction, sorrow and grief into the world. They are weakness and cowardice which were super charged by Antipas possessing power.

Now as the twenty-first century continues apace, we have heard ad infinitum an ill-defined term of opprobrium from the self-anointed guardians of us all, the progressive left. The phrase is "toxic masculinity," and presumably it is meant to denote, attack and ravage such presumed masculine traits as competitiveness, aggression, decisiveness and an ill-defined "macho" image of the male gender. Likely with some of the worst males the descriptive image is close to the truth when it attempts to define the male as a "brute beast," (by the way, a Biblical image), but only a willfully blind woman or man would deem all males to be toxic. Yet, there is such a quality as "toxic femininity," and both Herodias and Salome possessed it is abundance.

General observations may be made about the feminine that are neither prurient nor salacious. The Divine Plan and its Creator is fully aware of His own designs that women convey a powerful, sometimes overwhelming allure to men, and the heart and soul of that allure is physical. Girls, young women, and mature women realize such, but the good among them employs her charms with genuine emotion for the man she seeks to attract. The bad, a word itself not even emphatic enough to describe the immoral character of Herodias, wields beauty and sexuality as weapons to entrap a man or men in the web of her desires. Herodias may have her historical equals, but in this she has no superior. Enticingly beautiful herself she abandoned her husband Philip for Herod Antipas, whose political ascension seemed to be more assured. Philip was unceremoniously dropped, and in as clear a case of adultery as could be fashioned her union with Antipas was her political springboard to advancement. Not Herodias alone, though, because evil and sin, and their progenitor Satan, are never satisfied. Her young daughter Salome historically celebrated as almost the personification of budding and youthful sexual enticement was enlisted to help race the hearts of a group of older and powerful men. The scheme of Herodias worked to a point of perfection. She possessed the weaponry of beauty and position in her own arsenal, which was mightily bolstered by young daughter Salome, who was already mastering the talent of eliciting from the worst kind of men their worst instincts. Both Herodias, perhaps the New Testament's nearest equivalent to the infamous Jezebel of old, and the nubile young girl Salome truly were toxic. The results of the works of the flesh have been writ large upon the characterization of their historical personages, and they are led by adultery and murder. Herodias was an experienced virtuoso in making a mockery of her marital vows, and then elicited her own daughter as an accomplice in one of history's most infamous murders. Her life was a type of perfect memorial to the disasters which ensue when following the works of the flesh and violating most spectacularly the sixth and seventh of the Ten Commandments. Her victory, such as it was, over John the Baptist was short lived. Soon thereafter Antipas forever stained his soul and reputation by placing a crown of thorns and a purple robe upon Christ during His Passion. Both Herodias and Herod Antipas had reached the apogee of their success. Just a few years the insane Caligula became emperor in Rome, deposed Herod Antipas and gave his kingly title and throne to Caligula's friend, Herod Antipas I, who was the brother of Herodias. Antipas pleaded his case in Rome, but for his troubles he and his wife Herodias were banished to Gaul (now France) where they lived the remaining few years of their lives in exile. While king, one of Antipas's subjects was an obscure Galilean carpenter named Joseph, whose heart and action displayed the fruit of the Christian spirit and a true understanding of marriage.

Joseph

In 1751 the English poet Thomas Gray penned what is the most famous lyric poem in the English language or possibly any of the world's tongues. It is entitled "Elegy Written in a Country Churchyard" and itself is a strong current of sturdy yet crystalline beauty. The narrator is a man who is slowly walking through a typical English churchyard, which served as the burial ground, the cemetery, for the church's members. He observes the silent tombstones most engraved only with names too quickly forgotten but punctuated by their life's dates, and he wonders just who these anonymous decedents, what were their gifts and talents, their loves and losses but at the same time the poet writes in an air of melancholy, and is keenly aware that the world's summation of their lives is "the short and simple annals of the poor." The entire poem overflows with a linguistic and lyrical beauty that to its admirers is almost little short of unearthly yet it is this quoted line, above many, that possesses an almost unmatched literary and historical cachet. Even so great an historical figure as President Abraham Lincoln, when asked about his childhood and youth replied that it could be quietly summarized with the phrase "the short and simple annals of the poor." Such an epitaph is appropriate for the majority of the world's population, including a man born in the late first century B.C.

Joseph was the son of a man named Jacob, both father and son possessing names overwhelmingly common among the Jews. Stretching deep into past generations Joseph could assume pride in the knowledge that he was of the lineage of the great King David himself, but likely this was offset by the grim fact that Joseph was now a resident of the pathetic town of Nazareth, from which many thought nothing good could come, living in the bucolic backwater of Galilee. He practiced an essential, honorable and worthy yet hardly lucrative trade of carpentry. The "short and simple annals of the poor" was Joseph, yet he had a common desire of all young men, a young woman to be his wife and so settled upon Mary, a young maiden in Nazareth of similar obscure heritage. They were soon betrothed, and in ancient Jewish practice this seemed to mean something midway between what the modern age calls engagement and marriage. Each party was to remain celibate, including with each other, and simultaneously all others would still respect special bonds which they had with one another. In keeping with Mosaical Law tradition and cultural mores, it was a time and place of strict moral codes between the sexes, so strict that sophisticated moderns find them as easy to mock as they are difficult to follow. In all but the consummation of the relationship of Joseph and Mary, in the eyes of their families, friends and neighbors were already married. But then...

One night the angel Gabriel appeared to Mary in the famous Epiphany and informed the frightened and amazed young girl that she would give birth to a child, the Messiah, a prophecy from the beginning and one which had lain dormant for thousands of years. Mary's response was timelessly natural, being astonished she asked "how?" because "... I know not a man." As fraught with responsibility, heartache, joy and danger as it might entail, she was satisfied with the angel's response that she would be impregnated by God's Holy Spirit Himself. Mary, ever worthy of praise and adulation was happy, in phraseology of her own, to be "the Lord's handmaid." Still, she had a rough road ahead, a young, pregnant girl in a strict and strongly disapproving environment, but still she knew the blessing that had fallen upon her. This was not so, though, for a period of time for her betrothed, Joseph, who now bore a burden which would crush most men. Here he was ready to marry his love Mary and now a boulder had been dropped in the road before him. His sweet innocent bride to be was pregnant, and he knew he was not the father. He lived in a village with the tightest of moral standards, and as time progressed and the pregnancy became more obvious so would his shame and the moral obloquy and crude catcalls tossed in his direction. Joseph's dilemma was gargantuan, but in one simple gospel sentence his character was revealed:

> "Then Joseph her husband, being a just man, and not willing to make (Mary) a public example, was minded to put her away privately."

The Bible is a long record, extending through thousands of years of history, and it is not a record of cheap and easy compliments as to character. The very simplicity of Joseph's being called "just" alone is high praise for his character. A "public example" is a phrase as common today as ever, and endless multitudes of wounded spouses, sometimes even rightfully aggrieved, seek as much humiliation of a spouse that at one time could have been the object of their adoring, even idolatrous, love and passion. For the moment Joseph was hurt, even rightfully entitled to a belief that his beloved young betrothed had not betrayed him. But God allowed such a moment to pass in the twinkling of an eye. Before Joseph could act in any fashion, he, too, received a similar revelation from the God of Heaven. Again while sleeping an angel appeared to Joseph with those ubiquitous and ever comforting words from God to "fear not," for Mary's conception was miraculous and she was about to give birth to the Savior, of whom Joseph would be the father.

The scatterings of incidents in the four gospels reveal in Joseph the personality of a diligent, hardworking, quiet and above all, faithful man. The few brief moments of the lives of Jesus's earthly parents reveal that Mary was the one who would step forward and do the talking necessary. What we know of Joseph comes from a few Biblical snapshots and easily surmisable facts about his life. Like any responsible man he worked hard in a trade that doubtless demanded long hours and hard, physical labor. The financial rewards of remuneration were not abundant, but apparently, they were adequate for life in a tiny backwater village. After Jesus the gospels observe that Mary gave birth to at least six more children, one of whom, James, became famous in his own right. The New Testament rarely reveals the exact age of any person, man or woman, and neither Mary nor Joseph is an exception; however, we are informed that by the time Jesus began his public ministry at age thirty Mary was already a widow. On one place of understanding Joseph likely embodied much of Thomas Gray's apt reference to the "short and simple annals of the poor." To the world, ever blind or blinkered in its understanding Joseph is a long forgotten, obscure character, but to the committed Christian he is so much more and is worthy of the highest esteem. As Christ and His apostles taught so much of the Christian life is quiet, unnoticed, unspectacular, but shines with a radiance known but to God. Joseph was honored and esteemed beyond explanation by being entrusted with the earthly fatherhood of the Savior. Quietly but with a commitment that glorified God he was the masculine tutor and example to the Messian, the very Son of God who Himself forwarded Christianity with His own blood. Joseph lived before the actual founding of his son's Church, but in heart, deed and character his life of sacrifice, love, fatherly diligence and exemplary behavior proud that in spirit he truly was a Christian.

This section on Joseph opened with a quotation from Gray's "Elegy" poem, and likewise we close with one of even greater fame:

> "The paths of glory lead but to the grave."

For the world, for the non-believer sadly true. Because of Joseph, though, his special charge and vantage point and so many others, the path of Christ was prepared. With apologies to Mr. Gray, a man who himself wrote from a Christian perspective, Joseph more than did his part by showing through his son's life, death and resurrection that for the Christian the grave is not the end, but the beginning of the path to Glory.

CHAPTER FOUR

PERILS IN PERSIA

Finally in 587 B.C. the small, truncated kingdom of Judah after a long siege fell to the mighty Babylonian Empire and its great king and master Nebuchadnezzar. Earlier in 597 B.C. it had surrendered to Babylon and become its vassal state, but encouraged by Babylon's great western rival Egypt, the Jesus of Judah and its capital of Jerusalem had risen again in rebellion. The Babylonian rule now would be harsh and fierce and almost in a literal sense the old adage of "leave no stone unturned" was fulfilled. City structures were demolished and burned, much of the native population enslaved in the infamous "Babylonian captivity" and to the shuddering horror of the Jews the magnificent Solomon's Temple was destroyed, ravaged and looted of its treasurers. The Jews would now know the slavery of the magnificent Babylonian Empire and its ruler Nebuchadnezzar, one of antiquity's most noted despots.

Nebuchadnezzar ruled an empire which was attaining its apogee of not only wealth and power, but of opulence and decadence. Remarkably, even in the twenty-first century when Babylon as a political entity is entrapped in the pages of history books the name Babylon still resonates as a symbol and byword of unchecked riches and the deadening influence of soft frivolous living. It was, however, ruled by a man of considerable substance, for Nebuchadnezzar, although he reveled in his luxury and power, was observant, very intelligent and serious minded. He was also cruel and tyrannical, and the multiplicity of his personality and character elements seemed to always engage themselves in a strange personal civil war within the man. Nebuchadnezzar was all these things, and he was also very smart and astute in what he needed to govern an empire. The Jews of Judah he saw not as dead weight but potentially a great asset in bolstering his power and in governing his kingdom. He commanded that certain young Jewish men of aristocratic lineage, the sons of kings and princes be selected, thus:

> "Children in whom was noble rank, but well favored, and skillful in all wisdom, and cunning in knowledge, and understanding science, and such as had ability to stand in the king's palace, and whom they might teach the learning and the tongue of the Chaldeans."

Nebuchadnezzar desired the elite, the crème de le crème, to be an important cadré in the administration of the empire, and the Bible and history would prove him marvelously successful. These youths were to be favored with a royal diet from the king's own table, and after three years training and internship they would be ready to "stand before the king." Jews they had been, but their names were to by Babylonian, so Daniel, Hananiah, Mishael and Azaziah were to vanish in the wisps of history and become Belteshazzar, Shadrack, Meshach and Abednego. Biblically and traditionally Daniel's original name adhered to him, but the other three are forever known by their more lyrical Babylonian names. The king, doubtless unaware of the Hand of the young men's God, had selected the four with astounding wisdom. Bluebloods they were, but their characters would prove even more admirable, and the quiet, even gentle way in which they comported themselves would presage the "gentleness" of the fruit of the Spirit spoken of so much later by Paul. Nebuchadnezzar, too, was wont to be kind and gentle for he had found four young men to rise high in the Babylonian Empire. Aristocrats they were among their fellow Jews they would remain aristocrats among the Babylonians and even luxuriate in Babylonian wealth and a rich diet, which the four were commanded to be afforded. Here lay the rub, though, for Daniel and companions were observant Jews, strictly adhering to not only the moral but the dietary precepts of the Law of Moses.

The four young men were to be served daily the rich food and wine from the king's table, provisions that were likely somewhat unhealthy in themselves and likely in violation of the strict Levitical dietary codes. Daniel recognized the dilemma, the pincers movement between the desires of God and king, but threw no moral tantrum or rebelled against his lot. Instead, as chronicled by an instructive and beautiful passage:

> "Daniel purposed in his heart that he would not defile himself with the portion of the king's meat, nor with the wine which he drank: therefore he requested of the prince of the eunuchs that he might not defile himself,"

There in the cavern of the heart is the real battlefield of good and evil. Evil, the works of the flesh, is rarely defeated in the cacophony of battle but rather in the quiet resolution of the soul. In a long life, with great scriptural documentation. Daniel adhered to this resolution of faith in God. Not with clang and clatter did he defeat the enemy but with a calm and remarkably deep resolution of faith.

Daniel's overseer, a man named Melzar, was afraid for his own life if he had to report a rejection to the king. Daniel, though, proposed a type of unusual test, a ten-day experiment where the four Jewish youths ate their traditional diet and the "king's men" ate theirs. So agreed, and additionally God granted them the "knowledge and wisdom, and Daniel (even) had understanding in all visions and dreams." Nebuchadnezzar's favorable impression of the young Jews and their God grew apace until "... he found them ten times better than all the magicians and astrologers that were in all his realm." The boisterous threats of the heathen, theirs works of the flesh, the wrath of the idolators fell to the faith and gentleness of Daniel and his God.

The continuing story of Daniel, Shadrach, Meshach and Abednego, their trials, tribulations and triumphs is quite long in its richness of moral lessons wide and deep. Its full coverage is beyond the scope of this one chapter, but salient, crucial points of conflict illustrating the distinctions between the works of the flesh and the fruit of the Spirit are there for the taking, study and learning. For a time the glory, wealth and power of both Babylon and King Nebuchadnezzar continued to grow and to almost glow with its splendor. The self-image, self-satisfaction and ego of the king had little trouble in keeping pace:

> "Nebuchadnezzar the king made an image of gold, whose height was threescore cubits, and the breadth thereof six cubits: he set it in the plain of Dura, in the province of Babylon."

The mental image should be that of a blindingly extravagant obelisk, ninety feet by nine feet, perhaps resembling a somewhat miniaturized Washington Monument. Nebuchadnezzar, pulsating, throbbing and veritably bursting with pride, political and personal, set a scheduled day when "anybody who was anybody" in the kingdom would come and bow down in homage and obeisance to this graven image and, of course, to the king himself. These political acolytes included "... the princes, the governors, and the captains, the judges, the treasurers, the councilors, the sheriffs and the rulers of the provinces." Such grandeur assembled together had likely never been seen before in the empire. They were called not just to admire, though, but to render servile worship for:

> "... (W)hat time you hear the sound of the cornet, flute, harp, sackbut, psaltery, dulcimer and all kinds of music, you fall down and worship the golden image that Nebuchadnezzar the king has set up."

If not, the wrath of the king would befall any seditious miscreant and he "... would be cast into the midst of a burning, fiery furnace."

Likely little time elapsed before the sycophantic informants which plague all nations and organizations seeped out of the woodwork. They were Chaldeans, an important segment of the empire, who came and accused the Jews but not before the obsequiousness of lackeys:

> "They spoke and said to the King Nebuchadnezzar, O King, live forever."

Then they excitedly and likely gleefully related that three of his provincial governors, Jews who worshipped their own strange God, defied the king's edict. The men were Shadrach, Meshach and Abednego. Nebuchadnezzar in his "rage and fury" ordered the three rebellious officials brought before him. This royal semi-deity got straight to the point as the three men stood, seemingly browbeaten and ready to recant their presumed blasphemy:

> "O Shadrach, Meshach and Abednego, do not you serve my gods, nor worship the golden image which I have set up?"

So there this trio of alien Jews stood before the all-powerful king, himself backed by the putatively omnipotent gods of the Babylonians and upon penalty of an unspeakably horrid death were implored to recant their fealty to the God of Israel. Their natural talents, considerable as they were, had been augmented and honed by years of Babylonian training, were literally on the brink of being extinguished by one of the most painful deaths imaginable. The young Jewish trio had been favored but now they were being bullied and threatened by a king who seemed to live in a rage, and their response, calm, measured, that of men possessed of a Spirit greater than themselves ring out forever:

> "(They) said to the king O Nebuchadnezzar, we are not careful to answer thee in this matter.
>
> If it be so our God whom we serve is able to deliver us from the burning fiery furnace, and He will deliver us out of thine hand, O King."

Magnificent though the answer was immediately it was eclipsed by the words and sentiments which inspire faithful Christians yet today:

> "But, if not, be it known unto thee, O king that we will not serve thy gods, and worship the golden image which thou hast set up."

Such was and is the expression of the true committed believer, that God will do as the petitioner desires but even if not in His wisdom He remains the God of the Universe. Even a non-committed observer will likely make the observation that Nebuchadnezzar desired not so much the worship of his own gods but rather the worship of himself.

His rage was as white hot as he ordered of the fiery furnace, an intensity of flame not seen before. The king's strongest soldiers were ordered to bind the three recalcitrant young Jews and shove them into a fiery furnace made seven times hotter than normal.

Death by fire is the arrival of human suffering in one of its most horrid and intense forms. The fire itself quickly exhausts all oxygen, and the human sufferer attempts to gasp with an insane thirst for oxygen that simply has vanished into the conflagration of fire. As the heat intensifies and the flames furiously attack the body, literally melting the skin until its protection itself is vanquished, leaving but the vital organs to be piteously attacked and devoured. We may easily contemplate and surmise the accuracy and merits of that phrase "the fires of Hell." Nebuchadnezzar's rage and wrath, though, was if anything, hotter and more intense than the fires which he had prepared for Shadrach, Meshach and Abednego. Manhandled by the king's strongest soldiers the three men, already bound tightly, wrapped in their death shrouds, were hurled into the furnace of flame. So hot had the hellish cauldron already became that "... the flame of the fire slew those men that took up Shadrach, Meshach and Abednego." The three young Jewish men fell into the furnace but to the astonishment of the king and his company the three lived, but it was another that grasped the royal attention:

> "Then Nebuchadnezzar the king was astonished and rose up in haste, and spoke, and said unto his counsellors,
> Did we not cast three men bound into the midst of the fire?
> They answered and said unto the King, True, O King."

As astounding as was the survival of the three, though, it was another that captured the great monarch's attention and he spoke:

> "Lo, I see four men loose, walking in the midst of the fire, and they have no hurt; and the form of the fourth is like the Son of God."

The three young governors were completely untouched by Nebuchadnezzar's intended method of execution. The fires "had no power upon their bodies," and neither was their hair singed nor their persons bear the lingering smell of fire. These three gentle, kind, respectful and dutiful men had been saved by the Hand of God which insulated them from the flames of Satan's minions. The anger, rage and wrath of Nebuchadnezzar, the very essence of a work of the flesh fell to the faithful gentleness of the three young Jews.

Nebuchadnezzar, though, was the dangerous leopard who never changed his spots, and he now decreed that:

> "... any which speak anything amiss against the God of Shadrach, Meshach and Abednego, shall be cut in pieces, and their houses shall be made a dunghill because there is no other God that can deliver after this sort."

Violence, always wrath and violence from the king, but as for the protagonists of our story these self-possessed and God assured three young men were "promoted in the provinces of Babylon."

As the years elapsed Babylon continued to strengthen its power and reputation, and so did its king. Nebuchadnezzar was a violent and volatile man who never parted ways with the ferocious temper which he possessed. He was also a man whose sleep was continually troubled by dense, complex dreams which were an enigmatic puzzle to him. They were complex, and none of the magi, soothsayers, prophets or magicians for which Babylon was renown could make sense of them. So, at last the king sent for Daniel, by now a mature man, and by the inspiration of God Daniel was enabled to explain to Nebuchadnezzar that his dreams foretold the history of the world through the several centuries that were to follow, and how that the mighty empires of the Babylonians, the Medes and Persians, Alexander the Great and Rome would rise, flourish and fall, eventually giving way to the everlasting Kingdom of the Son of God. Nebuchadnezzar was so impressed with the reasoning, logic and clear-eyed preview of the future which Daniel's interpretation provided that the king placed Daniel over all Babylonian wise men and even over the province of Babylonia itself. Through it all, Daniel, who came to Babylon as a youth and was now a mature man manifested great self-control, faith in God and a gentleness of spirit, even in dealing with a man as powerful and inflammable as Nebuchadnezzar himself. Nebuchadnezzar, like all men, kings or common, was not fated to live forever in this world. At his death he was succeeded by his son (some say grandson), King Belshazzar. The new king provided one of the more notoriously infamous examples of a son succeeding his father in power and by his profligate ways losing everything his father had built. Nebuchadnezzar was a cruel, violent man, but for very evident and practical reasons he acknowledged the God of Daniel and offered a certain heathen respect to Him.

Belshazzar maintains a certain infamy well into the twenty-first century for hosting one of the most publicized parties of antiquity. This king hosted a feast, more realistically an extended debauchery for "a thousand of his lords" at which the wine flowed like flood water. Sufficiently supercharged with alcohol he ordered that the golden and silver vessels which his father Nebuchadnezzar years past the frivolity and gaiety of "... the king, his princes, his wives and his concubines." The sacrilege, too, flowed as freely as the wine:

> "They drank wine, and praised the gods of gold, and of silver, of brass, of wood and of iron."

The drooling guffaws of laughter and the uproarious revelry had crescended to its apogee where simultaneously:

> "In the same hour came forth fingers of a man's hand, and wrote over against the candlestick

> upon the pilaster of the wall of the king's palace: and the king saw the part of the hand that wrote."

Whatever the blood alcohol level in the king's system it suffered an immediate change and dramatic plunge:

> "Then the king's countenance was changed, and his thoughts troubled him, so that the joints of his loins were loosed, and his knees smote one against another."

Suddenly, in the face of a real miracle the great king Belshazzar lost control of his bodily functions and his emotions. "Fortunately" as he regained his composure he must have been somewhat comforted by the reality that he lived in Babylon, the world center of magicians, soothsayers and religious seers, and he demanded of them an interpretation of the writing and its meaning. At the very crux of their careers they all failed him for "... they could not read the writing nor make known to the king the interpretation thereof." As these great wise, but ineffective men, trembled in fear of the king's murderous wrath his queen remembered a man from the past, one Daniel, a Jew, who was remarkably successful in interpreting the dreams of the king's father, Nebuchadnezzar. Thus Daniel, long forgotten by many and but barely remembered by some, was reached and ordered to appear before Belshazzar and interpret the words which the disembodied hand had written on the wall.

Ever humble, noble and pious Daniel appeared before the king and was promised that if he could successfully interpret the writing, great splendor and ceremony awaited him and that he "... shall be the third ruler in the kingdom." Quickly Daniel waved away the splendid gifts of the king and spoke to him with a brutal reality which is seldom heard by kings. Daniel reminded him that his father, a man of superabundant pride and violence was so humbled by God that this king had literally lost his reason and lived for seven years as a beast of the field. Daniel continued and spoke the harsh truth that Belshazzar had never demonstrated a scintilla of humility towards God. Moreover, he had mocked the Creator by the desecration of the Temple treasures and was self-marked as a man unworthy of the crown. Finally, Daniel began his interpretation of the writing by simply announcing the words themselves:

> "Mene, mene, tekel, upharsin."

To-wit, you, Belshazzar, will have your great realm taken from you for God "has finished" your kingdom. It will become a portion of the massive empire of the Medes and the Persians, for you, Belshazzar "... art weighed in the balances and found wanting."

Certainly Belshazzar could not have been pleased, but he was true to his word, and had placed upon Daniel a scarlet robe and given the power of the "third ruler of the kingdom." As for Babylon and Belshazzar the mighty Persians had succeeded in diverting the barrier of the Euphrates River and that very night the mighty army of the Persian Empire marched into Babylon upon the drained riverbed. As a separate power mighty Babylon and its king Belshazzar were finished. All the treats, debauchery, violence and wrath of the Babylonian monarchs had eventually collapsed in the face of the calmness, gentleness and predictions of one of God's greatest servants, a man with the heart and spirit of Christ ever before Christ Himself had come to earth. The works of the flesh had fallen to the gentleness and righteousness of a "gentle man" and the man's God. The story has also given us two phrases that remain in common usage in the highly secularized twenty-first century, i.e. "the handwriting on the wall" and "thou art weighed in the balances and found wanting."

As for Daniel his transition to Persian suzerainty seemed to proceed flawlessly. The Persian Empire was one of the prime political entities of the ancient world and at its zenith contained one hundred twenty-seven provinces and stretched from Ethiopia in Africa to India in South Asia. It was exceptionally well organized and administered, and King Darius set over the provincial princes three presidents, of whom Daniel, now advancing into old age, was first in rank. Daniel was that rare man who grew not only older but wiser and even more adept. Long ago he had likely been a favored youth under Judah's King Josiah, had been rapidly advanced by the Babylonian King Nebuchadnezzar and then honored ever so briefly by his son, Belshazzar. The Persian Darius himself was so taken with the now aged Daniel's ability:

> "Daniel was preferred above the presidents and princes, because an excellent spirit was in him; and the king thought to set him over the whole realm."

How extraordinary had been the life of this one Israelite, taken in slavery as a young man and one who climbed up and down the greasy pole of leadership so many times and under so many regimes and rulers. He was now the most powerful and authoritative man, save for the king himself, in the entirety of the mighty Persian Empire, at that moment the greatest and grandest kingdom on earth.

All Persia was neither elated nor happy with Daniel as its ruler, and in fact the ruling class of the lords of the Medes and Persians shuddered at the thought of serving this aged Jew with his strange customs, and incomprehensible belief in one God only and a strange attachment and fixation upon inconvenient moral principles. Daniel was a wanted man who had to be destroyed and eliminated, but the Medo-Persian aristocracy knew this was no simple task. Daniel was highly favored by King Darius, and besides Daniel himself was no ordinary man nor ordinary politician as they wisely, or perhaps shrewdly understood:

> "But they could find (no) occasion against Daniel concerning the kingdom: ... they could no occasion nor fault, inasmuch as he was faithful, neither was there any error or fault found in him."

Sadly, it is the human condition that most people have the proverbial "skeletons in the closet," but politicians, public figures and rulers seem to maintain very large and burgeoning closets indeed. With Daniel and his long history the closet was empty, empty of self-dealing, bribery, disloyalty, dishonesty, sex scandals, etc. He could not be entrapped in the ordinary webs in which most ordinary men are trapped, yet his enemies were astute to grasp their one viable weapon:

> "We shall not find any occasion against this Daniel except we find it against him concerning the law of his God."

Venality and treachery almost always finds an avenue, and these vile, wrathful men, seditions to their own king knew that only with his religion could Daniel be destroyed. Their answer lay in that most common of all evils, the false employment of religion.

All the rulers of the kingdom, the presidents and princes, petitioned King Darius with the sycophantic salutation of "King Darius, live forever." Their net destruction which had been woven for Daniel is best described by the scripture itself:

> "The presidents, princes, counsellors, governors and captains have consulted together to establish a royal statute, and to make a firm decree, that whosoever shall ask a petition of any God or man for thirty days, save of thee, O king shall be cast into the den of lions."

In other words Persia would itself be monotheistic for one month, and thereafter its subjects could revert to the worship of any god they desired. In the interim this was a dagger poised to plunge into the heart of Daniel. The king, though, signed the decree.

But what of Daniel? How easy would have been the rationalization that for a mere thirty days he would remain silent and thereafter worship God as usual. Or he himself could have approached Darius and in anger revealed that this was no more than a nefarious plot concocted to destroy one man, Daniel himself. Daniel may have borne the burden of many years, but he found in those years the same temperament, the same devotion and the same faith which he had always possessed from childhood. Under threatened penalty of death Daniel comported himself as always:

> "(He) went into his house; and his windows being open in his chamber toward Jerusalem, he kneeled upon his knees three times a day, and prayed, and gave thanks before his God, as he did aforetime."

They had him, the king knew it, Daniel was likely braced for it, but God and some of his most magnificent creatures cast the deciding votes. The lion's den awaited Daniel, and the voracious ferocity of the regal animals, likely already half-starved, awaited. Felines, from domestic cats to such magnificent creatures as lions and tigers are fascinating creatures, and have many dedicated and loving admirers (a company in which the author proudly includes himself). The big cats, though, are natural predators and death from a pride of starving and woefully mistreated lions would be a gory horror to contemplate. King Darius himself passed the night in an agony of worry for Daniel, and in the morning checked his status. Almost delirious with grief Darius was greeted by Daniel who calmed him with the news that God had protected him, and the lions slept that night. The God of Daniel had "... sent His angel, and had shut the lions' mouths, and that they have not hurt me..."

Darius had Daniel extricated from the lion's den and now the king's wrath was turned upon Daniel's accusers. These men and even their wives and children were thrown to the lions and met the macabre, gruesome fate that had been planned for Daniel. Darius then issued a royal decree that the God of Daniel was, in point of fact, the "living God."

Over two and one-half millennia later the stories of these four Israelites, Shadrach, Meshach, Abednego and especially Daniel continuously thrill and awe God's disciples. Their detractors and mortal enemies yet stand as exemplary of the bitterness and tenacity of God's foes. Still all lived centuries before the earthly advent of Jesus Christ and certainly before the apostle Paul's instructions on the works of the flesh and the fruit of the Spirit. In the plainest of terms they were all pre-Christian, yet their lives beautifully illustrate the diametrical opposition of these two points of view. With underhandedness and venality the enemies of God sought to destroy His disciples, yet in their endless excretion of Satanic venom their works destroyed themselves. As for the four Jewish youths, all of whom matured into magnificent men they lived without knowing and seeing Christ, but their lives, like those of all the Godly at any time, exhibited the fruit of the Spirit.

Who or what this superb quartet of Jewish luminaries knew of the Holy Spirit is open for theological debate. Noteworthy of our attention, though, is a Biblical statement regarding Daniel at that time where King Darius selected him to administer the Persian Empire:

> "... an excellent spirit was in him."

And so it was, from youth to the final days of a long and incredibly productive life, often lived in the most difficult and antagonistic times imaginable. In the late 1100's and early 1200's lived one of the most famous figures in theological history, a man named Francis from Assisi, Italy. By every account he was a quiet, humble and very gentle man, eventually bestowed with sainthood by the Roman Catholic church and known yet today as the patron saint of animals. Whatever one's view of Catholic theology any fair-minded observer will be staggered and humbled by the many stories of the man's goodness. Once Francis remarked that "a Christian should always be preaching the gospel, but use words only when necessary." Daniel and his company lived before Christ, but their continuous and courageous manifestation of His Spirit was always a living sermon.

CHAPTER FIVE

ADULTERY, MURDER OR NEITHER

The vastness and expanse of history and the magnificent proliferation of races, ethnicities and cultures provide a variation in societies, mores and morals that is staggering in its range of practices and beliefs, of standards of morality and immorality. Still even among this panorama of miscellany certain standards and beliefs retain a common currency. One of these is that murder is bad, and most often in most societies and legal systems it is the ultimate violation of society's standards. Our presentation does not intend to be obtuse in any way, but to acknowledge and analyze "murder" a definition of the term is needed, and for this we offer a statutory definition from the criminal code of one of the fifty states:

> "A person commits murder in the first degree when that person unlawfully and with malice aforethought causes the death of another human being."

The statutes of the remaining forty-nine states may contain a word or two of variation, but in general not only America but the entirety of the world, especially the English-speaking world and even all lands that have been informed and influenced by the Judeo-Christian moral system will define murder essentially the same.

Many persons love crime stories and do so for various reasons. Some are macabre and gruesome, but others find an interest and satisfaction in seeing those guilty of such a horrible act as murder caught and hopefully punished. The murder aficionado is not lacking for resources in modern times, with the cinema, television, internet, books and most regrettably the daily news providing an endlessly replenished reservoir. Another, more ancient source more than holds its own in providing all nature and manner of murder stories, and this is the Holy Bible. The scriptures waste no verbiage in trying to justify cold blooded murder and especially in the New Testament and the coming of the Christian Age is the act seen as anathema and the very antithesis of "goodness." "Murder" and "goodness" are words that do not flow easily as partners in the same sentence, but in his Galatian letter the apostle Paul identified the former as a work of the flesh and the latter as a portion of the fruit of the Spirit. Murder, and goodness are the very pith and marrow of contrast, and examples of each are beyond plentiful in the Biblical accounts. In particular we offer four pairings of examples to illustrate the contrasts between murder and goodness, presumably the two extremes on the polarity of morality, but capable of being understood as two forks in a moral road in which different selections were purposely made by the protagonists.

Like all moral decisions the selection of murder or goodness ultimately is one of personal choice. Further, in the matter of murder rarely is it, then or now, a simple "clear" matter of murder alone. Murder usually is the final sinful and criminal act in a series of moral decisions which become inextricably with the homicidal act itself. The beautiful fruit of the spirit, goodness, is not as easily susceptible to a one-sentence statutory definition as is murder, yet in the end it is triumphant. The Biblical stories of contrast are abundantly plentiful, and we offer these four.

David and Joseph

This act is certainly in the competition for the dubious and most infamous act of adultery in all history and certainly in Biblical history. It is so well known that hopefully tedium will be avoided and as a synoptic expression of it is offered. Ancient Israel's second and most famous king was David, a multi-talented genius who was "a man after God's own heart." One evening, while his army which he commanded was in the field, he strolled upon the terrace of his palace and saw a beautiful woman named Bathsheba bathing herself. David's lust for this voluptuous beauty was aroused, and he summoned her to his monarchial bed where she, a married woman, and the king consummated the act of adultery. She was returned to her home and in the course of time discovered that she was pregnant by King David. Bathsheba's husband, a Hittite named Uriah, a captain in Israel's army, a man of proven bravery and loyalty to both God and King was away on duty in the field. David's scheme to quickly return Uriah to Bethsheba's presence collapsed due to the nobility of Uriah's character, and one route only did David now consider – murder. Adultery had led to a contemplated murder and on his route there David engaged in subterfuge, lying and ultimately treason to his and God's own kingdom. In the next battle and with the complicity of David's trusted general Joab, the loyal Uriah was abandoned and killed by enemy soldiers.

David's diabolical (and that is the proper adjective) plan apparently worked to perfection, yet nothing so horrible as murder, as iniquitous as it may be, can be performed in a sealed moral vacuum.

In the cuttingly curt words of the Old Testament account the aftermath of David's carnival of lust, duplicity and violence did not proceed in any devised direction for "... the thing that David had done displeased the Lord."

As David, now with a cold-hearted murder to his account, settled back into his kingly palatial life his trusted confidant the prophet Nathan came to visit him. He told the story of a pitiless rich man who killed the beloved pet lamb of a poor man so that this great man of wealth could revel in a party with his friends. David, king though he was, had started as a humble shepherd boy who cherished a special solicitous love for sheep and lambs still. Nathan brought him up short with those still famous words of "Thou art the man." The great sins of David, which culminated in the murder of an honorable man, Uriah, had been thrown into his face. It had begun with David being not with his army in battle but rather strolling on his terrace in the cool of the evening, a deliberate choice he had made. He saw the beautiful Bathsheba, likely wearing little or nothing, and his considerable desire had been stirred. His gaze lingered and his thoughts and libido went into overdrive, leading to her royal summoning to the king's bed and all that followed. To cover the sin of adultery he engaged in subterfuge to effectuate the return of Uriah from the battlefront, a scheme which failed because of the high, shall we say, "kingly" moral standards of Uriah. David chose to return him to the front and to be deliberately sacrificed in the heat of battle. David chose to place the sanctity of his own position above the life of a brave man and the good of his own nation. But David was certainly not alone in his possession of choices.

Through Nathan, David was told that he was deserving of death, but that He would spare his life. Instead the "sword shall never depart from your house," David, and the remainder of your life was to be a horror show of family miseries. All of this grew from David's choosing to stare and sexually devour an enticing young woman, which led down the wayward paths we know so well.

Very few men ever attain the ultimate ranks of political power or in point of fact, came anywhere near such. The same Old Testament, though, tells the story of another young man who lived many centuries before David and bore many substantial similarities to him. Joseph was the sone of the great patriarch Jacob and his wife Rachel. Jacob had twelve sons, and Joseph was the next to youngest. David was the youngest of eight sons born to a man named Jesse. Both David and Joseph have their stories emblazoned on the pages of the scriptures while each is still a teenager. David, of course, is introduced in the immortal story of his duel with Goliath and Joseph because of the fierce hatred and jealousy which his mere existence engendered with his ten older brothers. David was given a fast track to the kingship, but it was a track almost obliterated by problems and conflicts which with God's blessing he was able to overcome. Joseph's "track" seemed to terminate while he was yet a teenager, when the ferocity of his brother's hatred drove them to sell their younger brother into Egyptian slavery and a likely anticipated early death.

Many other tangible, even physical similarities, define any comparison between David and Joseph. From his youth onward David himself was an object of admiration for the fair sex, and here in the twenty-first century he remains a paragon of artistic male prowess. Girls and women adored him, and he reciprocated with the number of his total wives between eleven and thirteen. When Joseph went to Egypt as a young man it was not long before he captured the notice of females, for he is described as young, strong and though the word itself is not employed was certainly athletic. One woman in particular became entranced by Joseph, and therein lies our story.

Like David Joseph was unusually gifted, and the young man's talents were noticed quickly. Even though quite young and a Hebrew foreigner in a relatively short period he was appointed to be effectively the chief of staff to a man named Potiphar, a high-ranking official of the Pharaoh, likely the contemporary, most powerful monarch in the world. Not only did young Joseph possess all the physical attributes, for he "... was a goodly person and well favored" but his God-given talents were, if possible, even more obvious. So much trust and responsibility was vested in Joseph that Potiphar "... left all that he had in Joseph's hand, and he knew not ought he had, save the bread which he did eat." His passage from a teenager despised by his brothers, sold into slavery and stunning rise in responsibility is breathtaking, but well deserved. Potiphar knew a good man when he saw one. Unfortunately, so did Potiphar's wife, but for entirely different reasons.

Some with a sardonic pseudo-sophistication have claimed that Potiphar's wife (nameless as she remains) may not have been an attractive woman. Such an assertion should not be taken seriously. Although unlike Bathsheba, described as beautiful, this great Egyptian lady is absent a biblical description. Still, though, she was the wife of one of the most powerful men in the most powerful nation on earth, so it begs reasoned understanding to claim that she was anything less than beautiful and desirable. Her position and beauty bolstered her confidence, so one fine day when the house was vacant of Potiphar and all attending servants save Joseph so:

> "It came to pass after these things, that his master's wife cast her eyes upon Joseph; and she said, Lie with me."

Certain emotions and feelings are universally shared among all classes, all people, and from all stations in life. In a different manner but with the same intensity is the inborn sexual desire which is equal and many times surpasses the desire for food and water. It is unlikely that the desire for the opposite sex possessed with greater intensity and fervor than that belonging to a young man, and one such as our current subject Joseph. A beautiful woman has offered herself with all her feminine charms and delights to a young man, and what's more the episode presumably will be free of charge. Whether Joseph could "see this coming" or whether her proposition was sprung with total surprise is unknown. What is most assuredly known, though, is Joseph's magnificently and exemplary response:

> "But he refused, and said unto his master's wife, Behold my master worrieth not what is with me in the house, and he hath counted all that he hath in my hand.
>
> How then can I do this thing and sin against God."

Temptation contains within its definition a story, oftentimes an overwhelming strong desire to follow one's desire, heart or in Joseph's case, physical longing. Without engaging in a surfeit of cynicism let it be assured that Joseph for the moment found himself in a position of which the typical young man would dream and desire. For one moment of ecstasy he could drop all considerations of loyalty, both to his earthly master and to God, and revel in the pleasures this woman offered. Joseph had not searched for this moment, but here it was. A man a generation older, King David, may or may not have searched for that moment when his eyes found the delights of Bathsheba, but quickly he availed himself of her pleasures and began to extensively catalogue so many of the "works of the flesh." Joseph, though taken by surprise, found moral resolution at his core and exemplified the nature of a true Christian gentleman long before either of those words had been coined.

Joseph displayed the fruit of the Spirit in a situation recognizably similar to that which confronted David, and yet his reaction and behavior was a polar opposite. But which fruit? Sometimes a person's motivations and actions are difficult to define with a single word or term. Of those terms which Paul enumerated in his letter to the Galatians the most precisely descriptive is that of "goodness." Certainly it is a word which is prolific in the scriptures, and even in modern times its usage is ubiquitous. A precise definition remains elusive, though it may be found in the simple phrase of "a disposition to do good." Always, his entire life's story reflects that Joseph was imbued with this spirit to do good. Yet this does not mean that such a spirit crowded out from his character the temptation and the desire to do bad. A famous Genesis story later reflects that he was tempted to exact vengeance upon ten of his brothers, but that his good spirit led him away. Having a beautiful woman offer herself with the likelihood of a full panoply of physical and psychological pleasures most assuredly was a temptation that could have devoured Joseph. He resisted, and he was rewarded, although that reward was only in the sense of a very old and even rustic saying that "goodness is its own reward." For the moment Joseph's desires had to be sated with that since his goodness earned him a spectacular fall to the nether regions of Egypt. After all, he was still a Hebrew slave.

For the time being Joseph had to live with the reality that he was the best, even the most exemplary type of man, he had fallen prey to the worst kind of woman. One rebuff from Joseph was not enough for her and soon she found herself alone again with her victim. She caught Joseph by his clothing beseeched him anew to "Lie with me," but he pulled away with Joseph's clothing in her hands. Now humiliated she cried "Rape" and had Joseph's garment to prove it. She repeated his supposed crime to Potiphar, and his "wrath was kindled" and Joseph tossed into prison. For the present Joseph's rebuff of the great lady had shown the triumph of the works of the flesh over the goodness of the spirit, but the full story was yet to be told.

Our old adage proclaims that "goodness is its own reward" and so be it for Joseph. Now the rising star in Egypt had been felled, and he had to content himself with that reward. From a pinnacle of youthful fame, prestige, responsibility and comfort he fell, and from this precipice his landing was brutal and traumatic "... for Joseph's master took him and put him into the prison, a place where the king's prisoners were bound." From the zenith to the abyss, all because of the unsated desires of an evil woman, the gullibility of her husband and most of all the steadfast, unshakeable goodness of Joseph.

It is astounding the frequency with which old sayings, perhaps what some quaintly call folk wisdom, are proven true time and again. Our narrative of Jospeh fairly begs for the quotation of one, and that is "... cream rises to the top" or if the reader prefers "... you cannot keep a good man down." Just as Potiphar, a very important man, had entrusted his entire household to Joseph so did Joseph's abilities begin to impress even in the darkness and hellish nightmare of prison:

> "And the keeper of the prison committed to Joseph's hand all the prisoners that were in the prison; and whatsoever they did there he was the doer of it."

Though Joseph remained in the bonds of imprisonment:

> "... the keeper of the prison looked not to anything that was under his hand, because the Lord was with (Joseph) and that which he did, the Lord made it to prosper."

With the blessings of God, Joseph, at an exceptionally young age and in a foreign country, possessed a remarkable and well-deserved recognition of his abilities in that he quickly won the complete trust of his masters. Yet, he was still a prisoner, a young man bursting with extraordinary talents, remarkable energy and that quality so often difficult to describe, goodness. Yes, Joseph remained a prisoner, but so did others, including two men of noteworthy rank, the Pharaoh's butler and baker, who had incurred Pharaoh's wrathful and spiteful displeasure.

The two erstwhile important men of Pharaoh's court made the acquaintance of Joseph, and each related to him the substance of a dream which had recently tormented them. From the two dreams extracted two different meanings, each the polar opposite of the other. The interpretations so aptly and almost poetically rendered in the Book of Genesis led Joseph to two conclusions. Within three days the butler would be forgiven and restored by Pharaoh to his former lofty position, but as for the baker... within that same three days Pharaoh would take him, have him beheaded and his body hung on a tree for the birds to eat. Such came to pass and as the butler was restored to honor Joseph pleaded that he remember Joseph to Pharaoh. But in a display of humanity that is revoltingly common, and which would reach its nadir in the treatment of Christ, "... yet not did the chief butler remember Joseph, but forgot him."

Dreams have always been and show no signs of abating as openings to a world which is denied humanity driving its waking consciousness. They are fascinating, troubling, occasionally erotic, fanciful and more, but in the Old Testament God often employed them to reveal not only His will but also the future. The Pharaoh began to suffer troubling dreams, but could find none of the wise men, prophets and soothsayers of Egypt who could interpret their meaning. Now, only now when it was personally advantageous to him did the chief butler decide to remember Joseph. With the ingrained and practiced servility and obsequiousness of the career bureaucrat the butler approached Pharaoh, "... saying I do remember my faults this day," yet when I was in prison, I knew this young Hebrew with a remarkable talent for interpreting dreams. Thus Joseph was summoned and answered Pharaoh's call with the dream's interpretation.

Pharaoh was in no manner disappointed with the words of this magnificent young Hebrew. Joseph was honest to a fault, and he told Pharaoh that this great land of the Nile was to revel in seven years of plenty, which was the prelude to the suffering of seven years of famine. With the Divine knowledge of his God Joseph could easily point out the problems to come, great though they might be. Disregarding God's imputation of knowledge to Joseph (admittedly a gargantuan fact to overlook) it is easy to overlook that identifying problems is one matter. Competent physicians, lawyers, engineers, mechanics and service technicians and an endless array of others do this daily. What separates the merely competent from the good, outstanding and the great is that the latter grouping has the knowledge to give the solution to the problem. That Joseph had, and because of God's direction and His wisdom and goodness the mighty empire of Egypt would be spared destruction. The seven years of plenty would be sufficient to tide over Egypt through the years of famine if they planned and saved astutely.

Joseph' demeanor, youthful energy, reliance upon his God and the detailed authority and assurance with which he met the great Egyptian monarch so impressed Pharaoh that Joseph skyrocketed to heights undreamed of and rarely, if ever, so quickly in all human history. Pharaoh was so impressed that Joseph was made the governor, administrator or perhaps more precisely the prime minister of the nation of Egypt. Only in the power which was inherited and emanated from the royal throne was Pharaoh greater than Joseph. The rise of this next to youngest son of the great patriarch Jacob to his ultimate achievement politically while still a young man in his twenties has few parallels in all history. Although the two lived in different eras and different circumstances perhaps Biblically the man most similar in his meteoric rise in youth was that great figure with whom we have coupled Joseph's name in this essay, the young and ultimately the King, David.

David and Joseph are two of the most important men who ever lived. The greatness of each began to be revealed while they were still teenagers, and through long lives their spiritual stars usually shone brightly, and especially in the case of Joseph increasingly so. A descendant of David, Jesus of Nazareth, was never ashamed to refer to Himself as the Son of David, and

Joseph's character and historical lamination never dimmed among the Israelites. Both men came from good, though certainly far from perfect families. David was the very youngest of Jessee's eight sons, and Joseph was the twelfth of Jacob's thirteen children. Each followed God and followed enthusiastically while still quite young, and each was subject to violent opposition and vicious persecution from those who should have loved them. Through their own sterling and steely character each ascended to the top of their respective political ladders, and each even today is honored profusely by Christians. The greatness of each man is inexorably and incontrovertibly assured in this present world; however, the incidents that have been described in this chapter unfortunately illustrate the unbridgeable gulf between the "works of the flesh and the fruit of the Spirit" explained by another great man who lived long after the time of either, the apostle Paul.

God fashioned men and women so that the physical attraction of one for the other would be strong, very strong and in certain circumstances almost irresistibly strong. One evening David found himself besotted by the physical charms of a young married woman, Bathsheba, who was in the advanced stages of undress. Apparently, the king, who had already accumulated his share of women and wives could not resist the call of desired physical ecstasy before him. It would be too soft a term to say that David succumbed to temptation because he made no attempt to resist. His desire and Bathsheba's presumed consent began a course of nature that led to adultery, multiple lying, subterfuge, the disloyalty of King David to his own army and to his God and ultimately to murder. For a time the great man's life became an advanced seminar for the works of the flesh.

Joseph had presented to his desires a woman who was apparently insatiably desirous of him. A young man, in the burgeoning power of youthful desire she was standing there, his for the taking. Undoubtedly Joseph fully possessed the typical and powerful drives and physical appetites of the young man, but their satisfaction was not his primary concern, but instead that of pleasing God.

From the roots of the poisonous tree which David planted in Israel sprang not only his personal sins and deterioration of character but the beginning of God's dread sentence that "the sword shall never depart from your house." Opposition in his own family and civil war, seemingly endless, brutal civil war sprang up and became a fixture in Israel's history for centuries. Young Joseph's discipline and steadfast courage harmed him at the onset, but eventually God worked His will through Joseph, and the beginning of a great nation began to coalesce. The Spirit of God found rich soil in the soul of Joseph from which great fruit was grown. David, a man whose life's greatness still abides, travelled a road which appeared heavenly, but which made his life a version of hell. Joseph took the road less travelled and as the poet Robert Frost stated:

> "... that has made all the difference."

CHAPTER SIX

THE EXTREMES OF MODERATION

The history of humanity has demonstrated that hidden deep within the bosom and soul of much of mankind, individually and collectively, is a propensity towards the extremes in thought and behavior. From the Fall forward to the present the evidence is overwhelming that so many and much of mankind collectively is driven by ever increasing desires, even to the point of fantastic death wishes, in his behavior. In the Edenic nirvana in which the first couple was placed it was not sufficient that beauty, sustenance, authoritative dominion, endless pleasure and an eternity of existence was generously blessed them. Succumbing to temptation they desired the ultimate prize, i.e. to be as gods, thus being able to supplant their Creator. From this sin all others trace their lineage, but its immediate repercussions for Adam and Eve must be noted, for they, too, were extreme. Their innocence was lost; they were expelled from their Edenic paradise and landing in a harsh world were given the extreme hardships of pain, labor and endless trouble. From that moment onward man has been forced to live and transact with a world that often deals in a currency of hardship and extreme. Endless labor, pain, destruction, conflict, war, unhappiness and eventually death was ordained as the lot of humanity. Homo sapiens, though, is among other things, an endlessly innovative and creative creature, for men and women still prove remarkable in their seemingly innate abilities to ruin anything and everything into destruction as the logical ends of destruction.

Our examples of the above thesis may be taken from a gigantic catalog of man's abilities to find new ways to sin and displease God, but for the purposes of this one chapter we hope to focus only upon the abundant examples of extremes found in both the Old and New Testaments. Beginning with a thesis of this chapter, though, we may at times work somewhat in reverse in our exposition and explanations. God Himself notes many extremes, and His Word is never reticent in expressing the Divine opinion. The New Testament's most prolific writer, the apostle Paul, a man whose life's story was itself painted boldly with extreme colors and scenes, in our previously noted epistle to the Galatians, inventoried certain "works of the flesh" which may easily be inventoried as extremes. These include the sins of "drunkenness, reveling and lasciviousness" among others, and for each the scriptures provide endless examples of "immoral" substance which provide examples for why the Almighty detests such extremes. Concurrently the Bible will be neither stingy nor reluctant to demonstrate that in "moderate" form the activities which provide the fertile soil for these extremes of behavior are not necessarily sinful in moderation. These narratives, some quite famous, others to a lesser degree, should demonstrate that while some persons have always been ready, willing and able to the point of avaricious eagerness to plunge headlong into destructive behavior, others slip into a quicksand of destruction with little notice, at least in the beginning of their enterprise. Our debut view of the extremities of behavior provides the opening scene of one of the most famous and fascinating books of the Bible, that of Esther.

A Party in Persia

In the 490's B.C. Persia (the heart of which is now modern Iran) was itself a place of excess, beginning with its size and presumed power. It was an empire of 127 provinces which stretched from India in sub-continental Asia to Ethiopia in eastern Africa. It encompassed many nations, peoples and cultures, and in general was quite accommodating to the diversity of the cultures, races, ethnicities and religions of the massive number of different nations within its borders. Among those nations and people resided what was left of the nation of Israel, now reduced to a remnant of Jews who lived within the Persian Empire. In general this empire of gargantuan size was well administered and governed, and at its very zenith was an emperor. His was a position of enormous wealth, power and prestige and had already been held by major historical figures such as Cyrus the Great and Darius. The emperor as our story commences was Ahasuerus, more favorably known in western history as Xerxes. In the third year of his imperial reign Xerxes, at that time a young man, handsome, athletic, and known as a great horsemen, hosted a party which has had few, if any, equals in all history. We will allow the scriptural text itself to delineate the extent of its magnificence:

> "(H)e made a feast unto all his princes and his servants; the power of Persia and Media, the nobles and princes of the provinces being before him.

> When he showed the riches of his glorious kingdom and the honor of his excellent majesty many days, even a hundred and fourscore days."

Obviously, this was not a party per se for no group of even the most degenerate revelers could carry in for some six months straight. Likely it was more of an exposition or festival celebrating the wealth and glory of Persia and Xerxes.

Like all things in this world the great party, apparently a rousing success, finally came to an end. Yet, the feasting, drinking and conviviality was so sustained and so luscious that Xerxes decided to do it again, for soon thereafter he scheduled another feast for this group to be held in the court of the garden of the kings palace, perhaps as beautiful a locale of manmade beauty that was then extant on earth. Its walls were draped with beautiful finery of white, green and blue with this drapery being fastened with cords of purple and silver, all above floors of red, blue, white and black marble. This palace of pleasure and beauty bedimmed every other spot-on earth, but what is physical beauty without pleasure, and what can inject pleasure into any human gathering more quickly than alcohol. Thus, "... the drinking was according to the law, none did compel, for so the king had appointed to all the officers of his house, that they should do according to every man's pleasure." In other words, and in the modern vernacular "drinks were on the house." Undoubtedly, the alcohol flowed in rivulets, streams, rivers and tidal waves until all who desired were as inebriated as they likewise desired.

Xerxes, as emperor of the mighty Persian Empire, then the most potent and powerful on earth, was not shy nor was he hesitant in treating himself to the best of everything, and a best that came in massive quantities. The most powerful nation and army, the most beautiful home, the most powerful of friends and so much else of which he was proud, but his pride was not more greatly excited than that for his wife, the exquisitely regal and beautiful Queen Vashti.

On the seventh day of this feast when the king experienced the rush of his "heart being merry with wine," his royal masculine prowess got the better of him, and he commanded seven personal servants:

> "To bring Vashti the queen before the king with the crown royal, to show the people and the princes her beauty for she was fair to look upon."

This essay shall prove trustful and generous in granting to its readers full liberty to interpret exactly what Xerxes desired of Vashti. The setting, though, must be considered. All were gathered in this powerful emperor's breathtakingly beautiful palace and were on the seventh day of a high-level royal bender. Xerxes himself was a man whose power was hardly checked by an external earthly forces, he was young and would prove to be a major player in the history of antiquity, and he was besotted with his own power and importance and a voracious sexual appetite. Moreover, he was either drunk or well advanced on the road to that destination. It is unlikely that he merely wanted to showcase his beautiful wife so that his powerful friends and associates could complement her on the beauty of her dress. As we remarked, what Xerxes really wanted from Vashti is otherwise unspoken, but regardless the great emperor received nothing from his queen. Queen Vashti, whatever, whoever, however she was, at least has a core of self-respect and decency for "... the queen Vashti refused to come at the king's commandments... therefore was the king very wroth, and his anger burned in him." The subject of the relationship between the two (yes two) sexes continue to glow and flame with controversy still today. All men and women of any moral standard, though, should consent to certain basic principles, and one is that neither a girl nor a woman, a queen or servant, ancient pr modern, was created solely for the gratification of the male, be he prince or pauper. Vashti knew this, and for her infringement of her husband's command she paid dearly. Being the monarch of a great nation Xerxes had at his command the ability to transform his royal piques and whims into ironclad laws and here he did so:

> "If it please the king, let there go a royal commandment from him, and let it be written among the laws of the Persians and Medes, that it be not altered,
> That Vashti come no more before King Ahasuerus, and let the king give her royal estate unto another that is better than she."

This story, which is the introduction to the famous Old Testament book of Esther proves a marvelous example of how activity otherwise innocent is transformed into sin, and the works of the flesh by immoderation and excess. Banquets, feasts, celebrations, parties and the like are nowhere condemned in the scriptures, and their frequency is noteworthy. During His brief ministry Christ Himself was a man who came "eating and drinking" due to his frequency at social gatherings and events. A social event, a party or otherwise, offers no target for condemnation unless it is noted and characterized by excess. The self-worship, social tributes to Xerxes were truly exemplary of excess, though. They were excessive in length, extravagance, ego driven, self-absorption and all the effluvia that accumulate with such until they become what is condemned as a "reveling."

Reveling is a condition, a sin, which is similar to all other sins in many ways, not the least aspect being that it does not exist in isolation but is accompanied by other faults, some of which are more grievous than the reveling. No reasonable person, and certainly not Christ Himself, condemns having a good time, the jocularity among friends, the lighthearted harmless banter and so many aspects of conviviality that can overflow with a gathering of friends. What is beyond the pale, though, that which becomes a "work of the flesh" is the loss of good sense, judgment and the abandonment of standards of propriety which can lead to speech and acts of folly and harm. Here, Xerxes's exuberance and his overdeveloped youthful monarchial ego guided (or rather misguided) him down a rocky road of drunkenness and an attempted humiliation and degradation of his own wife, however desirable she may have been. We may aver with a certainty that historically and spiritually Xerxes gave no thought to the Biblically ordained Judaism of God's people and certainly not the eventual birth of Christianity centuries later, but nonetheless this powerful Persian ruler provides a potent example of reveling, always subject to Divine disapproval. By heritage, birth, his own royal environment and his ferociously insatiable desire for imperial and political power Xerxes certainly proved himself unfamiliar with the Christian spirit of "temperance" or "moderation" of which Paul wrote. Xerxes ruled a great empire for which many powerful never gave him obeisance, he was favored with a beautiful queen, and his royal word was law. In none of these qualities alone is there sin, but it was the attitude of haughtiness and overweening pride which allowed Xerxes to so transform them. Sadly and obviously the Persian emperor was far from the only monarch either Biblically or historically to be so inclined, but his story is one of the more illustrative of the principle that the abandonment of temperance will lead to dire consequences.

Samson the Superlative

The life of Samson is difficult to describe with mere pen and paper (or perhaps with a nod to the modern, a computer keyboard and printer), but in reality, it must be painted with broad, bright and dark coats of color. His short time in this world can be described accurately only by the generous employment of superlatives, unfortunately mostly bad. He was one of the final judges of Israel before that nation transitioned into a monarchy, and he remains one of its most, if not the most, famous, or at least notorious of the group. Samson was a large man of intimidating size, strength and demeanor so noted that yet today "Samson" is a synonym for magnificent masculine strength. Everything about Samson was oversized, including the negative, which unfortunately in notoriety has outweighed the positive. His physical strength was awe-inspiring and today remains a byword for male power, and he proved repeatedly that he was not a man to be taken lightly or mockingly by any. Unfortunately, so too were a vast number of his personal and moral characteristics were gargantuan in their dimension. Samson was personally boastful to the point of narcissism, often crude lapsing into obscenity and the vengeful. He once exhibited an inexcusable cruelty to a group of foxes by setting them aflame, all in vengeance to a group of men who offended him.

Samson was a man of God after a sort, but without a spark of flippancy let us assert that he was a man of women, many women, beautiful visions often, and just as often destructive of his character. Much as the teenage boy and young man of a certain masculine charisma he knew that the girls coveted his attention, which he gave generously and to a fault. Sorrowfully, for the sake of Israel and Israel's God the serious performance of his duties as judge always seemed to be entirely secondary.

As for his women the story of Samson and Delilah has never been confined to the Bible, but it has always exerted a large influence and the interest of any who hear it. Told and retold many times our essay will not add to the tedium of repetition by its repeated telling, but let it suffice to say that Samson was brought low and humiliated by this beautiful Philistine woman, and he cruelly suffered the loss of his eyesight and was forced with an animalistic pleasure by the Philistines to work as an enslaved beast. His life, tightly packed with many wasted years but certainly not without its heroic service to God, was one too often that of someone we associate with a modern athlete or entertainer, who cannot well manage the abundance of gifts he has been granted. Sadly, it is easier to describe Samson's life in terms of debauchery, drunkenness, cruelty and revelings, than to structure it around his sporadic outbursts of virtue. Finally, it ended with an event which strangely may be described as simultaneously his personal nadir as well as his dramatic apogee.

The Philistines, a longtime, almost hereditary enemy of Israel were having their own party when "... the lords of the Philistines gathered them together to offer a great sacrifice unto Dagon their god; for they said, "Our god hath delivered Samson our enemy into our hand." Our world has yielded many marvels through the centuries, increasingly technological in nature, but none has yet to be developed to register just how wrong a person or people may be. The Philistines, giddy with delight and many drunk with alcohol, were about to reach the heights of mockery as the blind broken down Samson, once the scourge of their nation was brought forth and placed between two pillars of the temple. It was not Dagon who had delivered Samson to them and their divinity, but rather the reverse. Samson in the final sacrificial act of his life, pushed and unmoored the pillars of the temple, and "... the house fell upon the lords and upon all the people that were therein, so the dead which Samson slew at his death were more than they which he slew in his life."

If ever the ending of a life could be acclaimed "bittersweet" it was that of Samson. From God he had at his birth been given extraordinary physical blessings, which most often he had converted into "works of the flesh" by his own self-regard and protracted immaturity. Samson's final act, though, had been introduced by his own last prayer to God when he had cried "... O God, remember me, I pray thee, and strengthen me, I pray thee, only this once, O God, that I may be avenged by the Philistines for my two eyes." The attentive Christian remains thrilled by the story, but admittedly he/she is made a bit uncomfortable by words of vengeance being on the lips and in the heart of the protagonist. Samson's life was too often characterized by Paul's works of the flesh, and our natural inquiry calls upon us where is the antidote Biblically. This chapter has touched upon such sins as adultery, murder, drunkenness, and the like, but where do we seek the opposing fruit of the spirit of temperance and moderation. Unsurprisingly, the words and deeds of one man provide the best answer.

Impetuosity and Narcissism Meet Gentleness and Moderation

An old adage, supposedly of Italian origin, reads that "if it isn't true, it should be." The applicability of such folk wisdom to Christ's famous parable of the prodigal son seemingly appropriate, but for all we know this most famous of stories told by Jesus and then related by Luke likely is true, the situations, characters and reactions being so genuine. Told so many time, including a fair input by this present author, we tersely summarize.

An obviously wealthy father had two sons, and the younger being headstrong, self-centered and just plain stupid demanded his share of his inheritance before he had done anything to earn it. The father, sad to see his son go, nonetheless gave him his share with which he scampered to a far country and there "wasted his substance with riotous living." Alone, beaten and scared, the youth decided to shirk back home, accept his father's disapproval and assume not the role of a son, but rather that of a hired servant. Christ's story reflects that the younger son had found the nadir of debauchery, working in a pig sty after days of revelry and drunkenness had ceased. In his brittle youthful mind he believed his father had the right to extract some vengeance but instead his father met him with the present of spiritual fruit, a loving, emotional welcome home, his exaltation, forgiveness, gentleness and love, pure, undiluted, untainted love. Among so many other things the younger son was immersed in gentleness and moderation. The true Spirit of Christ was proclaimed, no retribution, no rebuking and no revenge. The father, the parabolic representation of the Heavenly Father, demonstrated that moderation and temperance themselves and extremes, that is extreme forms of love. It is a model and ideal described and glittering with gold yet to the present day. Also in one beautifully crafted story Christ exposed and exploded the mythology that God is a harsh, vengeful Father, always seeking to "come down hard" on his recalcitrant children. In its description the Father's action is a wonderful paradox, for He had effectively gone to the extremes of moderation and temperance.

Jesus never shied away from parties and social gatherings, and in fact He admitted that His foes, the scribes and the

Pharisees, called Him a "glutton and a winebibber," both words being euphorically definitive. His cousin and predecessor, John the Baptist, was the opposite, a man who lived apart from people. From these two alone, the greatest of all prophets, John, and the Master Himself among the conclusions we may draw is that party and social participation are at the most very minor factors. Likely the most famous social date at which the Master was a guest was for a wedding feast in a town close to the Nazareth home of Christ, known as Cana.

Although two millennia separate us from the New Testament weddings, wedding parties, wedding feasts, etc., remain a large part of the societal scene in much of the world. In first century Judea they were incredibly important, and truly it was a time for celebration. The concluding word of the previous sentence, "celebration" is packed with abundant social, linguistic and even moral meaning. One of the premiere events in the life and ministry of the Son of Man occurred at this wedding in Cana, wherein it is often rightfully cited as the locale of the first miracle performed by Christ. As with His every thought and action, though, it contained multiple meanings.

Of course any person with even an elementary knowledge of the New Testament knows that this is where and when Christ performed His first miracle by turning the water into wine. For the thematic purposes of this work, though, may we examine this action as a representation of the Christian virtue of temperance, a word which not very long ago was associated with a commitment to the total abstinence from alcohol. The Bible itself provides a deep reservoir of stories of drunken revelries, as representative of works of the flesh, but what does it say about the opposite, the moderation or "temperance" concerning alcohol in its many forms and potencies?'

Much can be said in response to the question just posed., but for brevity's sake let us offer three major principles which the scriptures ordain concerning the usage of alcohol, principles practiced and taught by Christ. The first is that excess, wherein lies drunkenness is without exception condemned throughout the entirety of the Bible. Though we accept the scriptures as sole authority it should be observed that perhaps the majority of societies from time immemorial have condemned drunkenness and in many instances have fashioned the dictates of societal disapproval and even laws to so dictate. Public drunkenness, violence occasioned by excessive alcohol, and the general stupidity that is the offspring of its excessive usage remain, perhaps remarkably so, condemned in most settings and societies. A second principle is a recognition that any person who chooses not to partake in alcoholic consumption has made a wise decision which should not be questioned. That momentary relaxation, merriment, or in the ordinary patois "buzz" which a bit of alcohol may give its partaker cannot withstand the principles wisdom of its abstainer. The total avoidance of alcohol is a life's choice which is well known from the Biblical story. For instance the young protégé of Paul, Timothy, had to be encouraged by Paul to drink moderate amounts of wine for his "oft infirmities." Even more famously the precursor of Jesus Himself, John the Baptist, eschewed all alcohol. Nonetheless, history, the Bible and just common sense leads to the inescapable conclusion that the consumption of wine in moderation was part and parcel of the life of a disciple in the first century. Even before, no less a figure in Israel's history than King David long before had written in the Psalms that "... wine maketh glad the heart of man." None of this is in conflict, though, with the second great principle concerning alcohol. Simply, the man or woman who for whatever reason selects total abstinence has made a wise choice, and his decision cannot be gainsaid. Obviously, should one never consume alcohol he cannot be ensnared by drunkenness, alcoholism and the extremes of grossly negligent, puerile and even criminal conduct which it may engender.

The third great scriptural principle concerning alcohol is the one likely packed with the most contention and remains unaccepted by many sincere, committed Christians. The moderate, temperate consumption of alcohol is condemned in neither the Old nor the New Testaments. The biblical record, which covers a span of over four thousand years almost always invokes God's words of warning, but not condemnation, concerning alcohol. Obviously, situations arise daily that dictate that a person should totally abstain. The examples are obvious as they are endless. No physician should partake before performing surgery, driving a car requires total sobriety and perhaps even most importantly the conscientious expectant mother, without exception, eschews the use of alcohol.

Back to the wedding feast at Cana. A Jewish wedding feast of the first century could be an event surpassing even one day at length, somewhat akin to a come-and-go party. The best wine was served first and whatever remained was given to the guests amid the certain fall of the wedding celebration. As He so often does Christ reversed man's thinking on the matter. His own mother, Mary, informed her son that the hosts of the wedding feast had run out of wine. Christ then for his introductory public miracle, turned water into wine. All found that, astounding though it may have been, the Master had saved the best for last. It is ludicrous that the God who without exception condemns drunkenness would have been the progenitor of it at this wedding feast. All the guests were amazed by the timing and the quality of the wine, and with happiness they departed the wedding celebration.

The contrast with Christ's employment and partaking of wine, especially in ancient times a beverage of very limited alcoholic content, is a contrast with so many Biblical parties that it literally brandishes the wisdom of temperance with the "works of the flesh" found in the drunken Bacchanalians of such figures as Balthazar, Xerxes and Herod Antipas. One of the lodestars in the Christian firmament is moderation, for again as Paul said, "Let your moderation be known in all things." From the outset the scriptures have taught, and every moment of his life Christ lived and demonstrated the principle of proportionality. Some things are, in fact, more important than others, and what may be taken in moderation becomes poisonous and deadly in extreme.

The lives of those discussed, those language figures such as Belshazzar and Herod, had no concept and no desire to practice moderation. They destroyed themselves with excess, not just that of alcohol, or even sin but an excess of their own desires which could never be sated. The simple follower of Christ knows the importance of all things, including their relative standing in life, and by character and personality the fruit of the Spirit is so observed. Whether he/she is even aware the personal character and reputation is being formed, perfected and shown to the world. The scriptures, as does life itself, provide an abundance of examples where alcohol is central to human behavior. In the twenty-first century it so remains, but the mature Christian is destroyed not by alcohol but by excess. So much of earthly existence and the price of this world entangles a person and pulls the body, mind and soul into the dangers and destruction of extremes. That of the Father and of Christ instead is but another, an opposite, the extremes of love and the temperance of conduct.

CHAPTER SEVEN

HERESY AND FIDELITY

"Heresy" and "heretic" are words which many moderns, especially those of an irreligious disposition consider old-fashioned, even archaic, and to be honest, subjects of taunting and mockery. In traditional usage and in its purest sense heresy is the total rejection of religious orthodoxy, tradition religion and morality and in particular Christianity. But what if religious orthodoxy itself is passé and the subject of mockery of the intellectual and societal sophisticates along with the vast hordes of ordinary, common people? If no one practices orthodoxy how can anyone be a protester, a recalcitrant misfit, or i.e. a heretic? With the apparent and at times massive decline of so-called orthodox Christianity in the late twentieth and early twenty-first centuries such arguments are not inducive of quick disregard. With no orthodoxy can there be a heterodoxy?

But ... orthodoxy yet exists and is even supremely regnant in so many sectors. Especially in Western society, an orthodoxy of thought exists in most intellectual circles, academia, entertainment, in much of the judiciary in most places, business circles and the shapers and movers of the actions and thoughts of modern society. It is an orthodoxy that rejects notions of traditional concepts of God for various forms of atheism and agnostism, which themselves are breeding centers for materialism and hedonism. It is an orthodoxy that fancies itself as magnanimous but is in fact, the harshest and most tyrannical of forces when it comes to any discussion of morality, race, ethnicity and gender (a word which somehow has become a replacement for "sex"). To violate this code of orthodoxy in action, speech or even thought is to court the fiercest retribution of the keepers of this modern orthodoxy, which is usually referenced as "cancellation," becoming a person whose thoughts and opinions go unheeded and is deliberately ostracized from the orthodoxy which self-supposedly thinks and acts on a higher moral plane. In action it can be breathtakingly harsh, and in the name of "progress" it is an orthodoxy as harsh as any religion which preceded it.

The point of this introduction, hopefully made, is that orthodoxy is always existent and probably always shall be. Like many things in our world it can be anywhere on that scale from very good to very bad. Orthodoxy, although a word never employed in the scriptures, is usually accepted and presented approvingly as the standard of belief, obedience and conduct which God expects from His people, be they Jew in the Old Testament a Christian in the New. Though the word orthodox may be employed the term "heresies" certainly is, inasmuch as Paul listed it as one of the works of the flesh. "Heresy" is common usage has customarily come to mean a deviation from orthodox practice; however, the Biblical content of its employment rather indicates not merely a deviation from orthodoxy but rather its rejection. Both Testaments contain an abundance of heresy, and it is a practice which began shockingly soon after Creation, and it is to that first example we now turn.

The original orthodoxy which God planned for humanity was, among other things, perfect. In Eden, Adam and Eve were given perfection in the form of beauty, plenty, loving care from God, companionship and human love, the friendship, warmth and innocence of the world of animals, and it was for eternity. Adam's work was, in fact, delightful as he was given the responsibility of naming the animals, and over it all he exercised dominion. The first couple were literally given the run of the garden and were to even be unhampered by the singular commandment that God gave them, concerned the tree of the knowledge of good and evil, from which they were not to eat. This was the original orthodoxy which God provided for His creation, and it was an orthodoxy to be unavailable elsewhere other than at the gates of Heaven. It was literally the Edenic perfection, but its days were but few, as that great progenitor of heterodoxy introduced himself into the world.

One day that most cunning of all beasts, the serpent, appeared to Eve. We should not think of him in the manner of which we now think of snakes, but rather as subtle, charming and even beautiful. The serpent (Satan's) first recorded words were in the guise of a rhetorical question:

> "Yea, hath God said, Ye shall not eat of every tree of the garden?"

Eve responded with the answer Satan already knew, which was yes except for the one tree which was forbidden. Satan was given the stage, and he responded with the world's initial, greatest and longest lasting heresy:

> "Ye shall not surely die:

> For God doth know that in the day ye eat thereof, then your eyes shall be opened; and ye shall be as gods, knowing good and evil."

With this masterfully synthesized lie and half-truth, heresy was born. The true orthodoxy of God is His people (which He designed to be all people) content, innocent and living in Divinely eternal pleasure and protection. Satan raised the stakes with illusory promises of his version of eternal life and humanity's ascension to god status. The obvious and natural inference is that if men and women are themselves gods why do they need the God who created them? The first heresy, and the tree from which all mankind's problems and sins forever are traced.

Cautionary is the word that must be employed whenever we attempt to place motives, thoughts and words into the mind of God. Even more so should this be a watchword when we attempt to do the same with Satan. Nonetheless, though, in view of the fall of man and his subsequent history of self-degradation an offering of supposed insight into his thinking is here made. "How easy that was" Satan must have thought. God, his arch-enemy in Heaven and now earth and before the beginning of earthly time, had been bested and beaten with the simple inducement of that most supposedly noble of His Creation, man. Satan must have thought and or perhaps oven known that the celestial playing field had tilted in his direction. If God's first human creations could be corrupted so willingly and easily the remainder to follow would topple like the blowing of chaff in the wind. Adam and Eve were heretical and rebellious towards their Creator God so why should not their offspring and lineage forever more? The eternally sad truth is that Satan was right, and for God to overcome the triumph of the prince of darkness

His plan of redemption had to follow. But that story, the greatest of all, must be deferred. For the moment and as much as could be ascertained darkness and heterodoxy had the field to themselves. The orthodoxy of God, the true orthodoxy and not man's twisted conception of it, lay and yet does, in the simple obedience to simple commands, all within the loving purview of Divine Grace.

So where did this initial heresy of the human succumbing to the temptations of Satan lead? Seemingly, for a thorough exposition of the answer to this question a protracted study of the history of the world is required. But not really. Heresy, whatever dictionary, seminary, pulpit or theological, definitions may be given to the word, actually is humanity's decision to walk in their own footsteps because, self-acknowledged or not, they concede that they are gods. This is the history of the world, played out in all eras, in all continents and climes, and by all races and nationalities. Doubtless our early ancestors did not think in such specificity, but a later great prophet Jeremiah did, who explained that:

> "I know that the way of man is not in himself: it is not in man that walketh to direct his steps."

True heresy lies in the mass of humanity not knowing, caring about or in any manner grasping the great truth expressed by Jeremiah. From the Fall men and women in all eras, situations, kingdoms, republics, empires, etc., have spoken in terms of independence, independent thought, independent actions and so forth. Much, although not all of it is mass disingenuous for most people want and need some direction, some purpose in their lives. Independence and individuality are good at times even marvelous conditions, but from Eden forward anyone fools himself if the belief is adopted that they are complete free agents. The atheist, the agnostic, the deist, and so many other self-deluded persons may sincerely believe their lives and souls, if they cling to this admittedly doubtful belief, are independent. The wise person, the obedient, the good, sees herself not as a free agent but the child of the Creator who possesses the Divine spark of eternal life. This is true orthodoxy. The heretic finds no independence, no matter how firm he may be in his delusions but rather chooses the heterodoxy, confusion, and continual confession, chaos and change of servitude, the slavery for which Satan is the master. Adam and Eve and the endless multitudes which still follow in their moral choices have not become as "gods" but rather the pets and toys of Satan. This is true of that host of Biblical villains, terrors with power though they may have been, from Pharaoh, Ahab, Jezebel, Herod, Caiaphas, Pilate ad nauseum. It is true of the great philosophical and political intellects of all eras, men such as Rousseau, Marx, Nietsche, Sartre, who have gloried, however brilliantly, in their own ideas and intellects and the enormous influence for diabolical destruction their varied ideas have wrought. As influential as they have been and remain, as smart, as brilliant, as far-reaching and iconoclastic as their doctrines remains their heterodoxy is itself an orthodoxy. The more independent from God the human mind becomes the more its dependence and allegiance to Satan increases. The Devil knows this, has always known this and recognizes perhaps that when mankind becomes enamored with his own heresy and independence from God the more dependent upon Satan he becomes. Although the word is anathema to most who practice this, they in their intellectual, moral and fashionable pretensions are with their heresy the foremost practitioners of orthodoxy, the orthodoxy of Satan. To place this in historical terms a reference is made to the famous twentieth century poet and essayist T. S. Eliot, he averred that if you do not bow to God, and He is a jealous God, you must pay your respects to Messrs. Hitler and Stalin. This is not to assert that all unbelievers are as deeply and morally corrupt as such historical monsters but rather to aver that the only true orthodoxy is in obedience to God.

The tales, legends, metaphors and histories of heresy may have had a beginning, but seemingly in their ever-increasing darkness they have no end. Perhaps, but perhaps not, and now we turn to faith, or perhaps more specifically "fidelity" which is the beautiful fruit of the Spirit resting in opposition to heresy.

Fidelity

A Roman centurion of the first century in this faraway province of Judea was a mighty man indeed. For a long time as Rome, this city on the Tiber River, was slowly rising to power, he was both the symbol and reality of Roman power and military might. Ordinarily, centurions came from the equestrian class, a fairly low-level rung on the ladder of Roman aristocracy, perhaps roughly akin to the knighthood rank in the old but still more modern British class system. For generations he received his title of centurion because he was the commander of an army century of one hundred men. This was numerically altered early in the first century B.C. when the powerful Roman official and general Marius restructured and reformed the Roman army resulting in a century's reduction to eighty legionaries. Regardless of the number in his command, the average centurion was intelligent, well-trained, experienced, and a hardened soldier. Even two centuries hence historians recognize centurions as the backbone of the Roman army. Doubtless they were tough, powerful men and in their generally powerful and capable hands they wielded the might of Rome. At the time of the New Testament it is likely that most were Roman or Italian by ethnicity. A centurion thus was Gentile, pagan by birth, pagan by training and most likely pagan to the core. He and his ancestors paid homage to a pantheon of gods and goddesses that were themselves often brutal, deviant and at least as flagrantly immoral as the worst of humans. The Jews' Mosaical Law and now this young teacher from the nowhere of Nazareth likely would make little positive impression on the average centurion. Yet...

On a day fairly early in his ministry Jesus was teaching and healing in the Galilean village of Capemaum, effectively the Master's adopted hometown. There Christ was met by a Roman centurion and/or his servants and soldiers who besought the Master with a type of story which Christ would hear so often. The centurion's beloved servant was desperately ill and close to death. The usually powerful centurion was hopeless and helpless and could do nothing to save the servant except for placing the matter in the hands of the Master Himself. Christ, ever moved to compassion assured the Roman that He would come and heal the servant. Jesus now was met with a reaction of such deep faith and fidelity that two millennia hence and forever more will it stun the reader, even as it did with Christ Himself. No, said the centurion who instead replied:

> "I am not worthy that thou shouldest come under my roof: but speak the word only, and my servant shall be healed."

As startling as was this soldier's faith, he also revealed a quality that is just as rare, that of a man with authority who understood its proper usage and its limitation, as he spoke:

> "I am a man under authority; having soldiers under me: and I say to this man, Go, and he goeth, and to another, Come, and he cometh; and to my servant, Do this, and he doeth it."

The centurion's faith was startling and was from his heart and expressed with incontrovertible logic. He, an admittedly powerful officer had the authority and power to order men to perform the mundane daily tasks of soldiering and daily life itself without his physical presence. Why, then, should the personal presence of the Son of God be required for a miracle of Divine healing?

Christ "marveled" and exclaimed that He had not found this type of faith, this fidelity to His teaching and authority in Israel itself. From that moment forward, this servant of this centurion, was healed, and the Roman's faith and fidelity to the person and teachings of Jesus Christ was well rewarded. Since Christ was often prone to make this type of contrast so shall we indulge. Much later in His ministry the Pharisees together with their traditional foe the Sadducees "... tempting desired Him that He would show them a sign from heaven." Daily the Master was performing miracles, He was continually fulfilling with astonishing perfection Old Testament prophecies, and His life itself glowed with the radiance of the Son of God. Still, these learned scholars, theological intellectuals and presumably wise men steeped in Jewish law and tradition sought a sign. Aith does not spring alone from knowledge, and for some they commit the ultimate heresy of rejecting Christ. This Gentile centurion, though, needed a short exposure to Jesus to know that He was the Christ. We regret that he thereafter does not appear in the New Testament chronicle, but the enduring faith of a very great lady is told over time.

The story of a young woman named Mary from the Galilean village of Magdala has long been an inspiration to faithful believers and we daresay an enduring story of fascination even for many non-Christians. For two thousand years many legendary, even fanciful tales, have been engendered and retold as gospel to where she is a woman whose personality and image has been buried under supposition. Biblically, though, she receives her introduction as a woman somewhere in Galilee who is plagued by the possession of seven demons, a livid and regretful condition of some frequency at the time of Christ. The Savior encounters Mary, exorcises her of the demons and from this point forward she becomes one of, if not actually th most faithful of all Jesus's disciples.

In gospel accounts she is invariably included by name in that troupe of disciples and apostles, women and men, who accompanied Christ in the itinerancy of His teaching work, and her discipleship appeared to include financial contributions to the work. Plainly and with beautiful simplicity it may be proclaimed that wherever Christ went there also went Mary. Likely she herself was a teacher of notable merit as a daily observer and adherent to the Master Himself.

Part of the definition of faithfulness and fidelity is the factor of longevity. A person who takes a few steps forward in the youth of a popular cause and the plaudits of the crowd but then turns away at the early stages of opposition is hardly a paragon of fidelity. It is stirring, heartwarming and inspiring to proclaim that Mary Magdalene was the opposite of such a disciple, for she was truly faithful to the "true" finish. This is not the forum for a retelling of the events of the Passion of Christ, but let us aver the obvious that a portion of Christ's sufferings was that He was denied, forsaken and abandoned by most of even His closest disciples at the time of His agony, suffering and death. The gospels record that at the death scene on Calvary only three of His closest disciples remained. They were his own mother Mary, His especially beloved young apostle John and Mary Mgdalene. The killing ground of Calvary was a dangerous place to be, and many otherwise faithful and intelligent disciples of Christ held the knowledge of this fact in the grip of their own fears. As for Mary the love of a good mother is a quality to be recognized as almost closer to Divine than to mortality, and Mary has for two thousand years been deservedly idealized as a mother whose character is to be emulated, deservedly so. John was the "beloved" apostle of Jesus, the young disciple who had a special personal bond with the Master and took his faith and love all the distance to the dangers which lay at the foot of the cross.

But Mary Magdalene? What made her such a special and faithful disciple that she was at Calvary, and as we are about to recall went even further than that? Truly only God knows, but certainly we may be permitted commentary on what we actually knew. Her faith was of a quality that she witnessed not only the ghoulish macabre crucifixion of the Son of God but also His burial. By this point even the beloved apostle John was absent when the body of Christ was taken for burial in the tomb provided by one Joseph of Arimathea. His body was placed in the tomb, and the burial itself observed only by His mother Mary and by Mary Magdalene.

Like all the disciples on that Friday the emotions of Mary Magdalene must have been a dark, whirling maelstrom. Suddenly, the man upon whom the very meaning of all existence they had centered was crushed and placed in a borrowed tomb, apparently to their thinking to be but a memory. Burt Mary Magdalene was a faithful friend and disciple to the end. After enduring the likely hellish gloom and Stygian darkness of Saturday Mary and several other women before dawn on Sunday morning went to anoint the body of Jesus with oils and spices, a custom of Jews. (Without making a wandering side-track we here note that so often it is women who will take the paths of discipleship further than men).

All four gospel writers give an account of what later came to be called Easter Sunday, and each of them should be consulted and studied for the information each adds to the matrix of the story. Their first great shock was the finding of the empty tomb, at the front on which rested a giant boulder which had been rolled away. Soon news reached the apostles, and Peter and John came to the Garden to discover the source of the commotion. The two apostles ran, and John reached the tomb first, Peter following, and both bewildered when they saw an empty tomb bereft of everything except a burial shroud. Stunned and shaken they left and went back to the other apostles, and Mary Magdalene alone was left. She was devastated with the horror of the events of the previous days, and now she was bereft of even the body of Jesus to honor. The emotional catastrophe of the past three days had overwhelmed Mary. Weeping, she looked into the sepulcher and saw two white clad angels sitting at what had been the head and feet of Jesus. The angels asked the reason for her sobbing, and she told them and left the tomb. The stage was cleared, the cast in place and the moment set for both the greatest dramatic moment this world has yet seen, and the greatest earthly prize ever given to the faithful believer.

Even though it was a place of sadness and contemplation, this ancient cemetery was quite pleasant on this early spring morning. It was that time of the day when the blackness of night is in retreat and is surrendering the promises to the opening of a new day, but this time a day such as this world had never seen. A phrase of two millennia hence would extol this as the "dawn's early light," delightfully cool, soothing and comforting mankind, except for a relative few then and now, never grasped what this dawn was bringing. This young woman, Mary Magdalene, so beautiful in so many ways, was honored to be the first of the few. After speaking with the two angels she turned away, and in the yet dim light of the dawn saw another man, presumably the gardener or groundskeeper, standing but a few feet away. He asked her the simple question of "Woman, why weepest thou? Whom seek thou?" Mary, supposing her inquisitor to be the gardener, simply asked where the body of her Master had been taken and lain. The dramatic tension was broken, and the glory of the moment was given when Christ spoke but one word to her, "Mary." She turned, faced Him and with a voice undoubtedly clinched with passion and awe herself replied likewise with but one word, "Master."

The promises of thousands of years, the redemption of humanity and the destruction of death itself finally had come and had come and been revealed in the coolness of aspiring morning first to an otherwise unknown young woman. What had been prophesied and promised by God Himself to great and historically famous Old Testament figures of the stature of such as Abraham, Isaac, Jacob, Moses, David, Elijah, Jeremiah and so many others had its glory first revealed to a non-descript lady of the village of Magdala. As the scriptures themselves had enunciated this once demon tormented woman had been made whole by her faith, a faith obviously driven by love, and it was she Mary Magdalene, who first saw the risen Christ. A greater honor in this terrestrial realm is impossible to imagine.

The theme of this chapter has utilized the juxtaposition of two distinctly different concepts, heresy and faithfulness, which itself seems somewhat of an oddity. Other examples of both heresy and fidelity could be employed, but these three seem sufficient to illustrate the opposing poles of thought and living discussed by Paul. The Roman centurion and Mary Magdalene were each unlikely exemplars of faith. The centurion was a powerful office in a Gentile army which spread the grandeur of a civilization which at the time had no regard for the Jews's monotheism and strange laws and moral code. Yet he was convinced by evidence and both declared and followed through in a belief in Jesus as the Christ. The faith and fidelity of both Mary and the centurion received their immediate earthly rewards. Before the skeptic proffers his argument, we willingly admit that individual acts of faithfulness often, if not usually, have no immediate rewards. We walk by faith, not by sight, but it would be impossible to find a believing, practicing Christian who has not experienced an abundance of specific rewards for faith.

This essay has spoken of only one heresy. Heresy is a very serious matter, and the history of the Church for two thousand years has proven so. In the Christian Age its first manifestations are shown by the text of the New Testament. Apparently, the Church's first real battle with heresy was in its form of "Gnosticism," a compilation of ever-changing doctrines that remain today and whose thorough study demands a work of almost encyclopedic length. Since then Church disagreements have been as Abraham's abundant seed, i.e. endless, ranging from the proper approach to music in the Church, various positions and issues of church governance, worship positions and issues of church governance, worship practices and the end is just that, endless. Some ideas are, in fact, heretical, but many are merely differences between various faithful Christians. Shall we not place real heresy to the charge of that first and greatest of all heretics, Satan, who has never lacked success in convincing man that he may substitute his will for that of God's.

It is a faithless practice, and its ultimate reward is the sharing of eternity with its first proponent.

CHAPTER EIGHT

HATRED AND PEACE

The Master Himself affirmed that there will always be "wars and rumors of war," and true as it was in the first century the next two thousand years history have done marvels to highlight the veracity of Christ's statement. Even intelligent persons of a non-historical bent know that one of the salient truths of history is that mankind has navigated its rough currents and has been pushed forward, backward, sideways, up and down by nations at war, and wars which at times brought peace but often ushered in new wars and new hatreds. In the century just past it is now accepted as almost holy writ that the hatreds which engineered the bloodbath of World War I also prepared the world's stage for the even greater cataclysm of the Second World War.

Although it is in no sense a secret or undiscovered truth of less historical recognition is the fact that most nations, almost all in fact, have experienced the internal disasters of civil wars. In the modern era such large and influential nations as Spain, Russia, China, India/Pakistan, and likely the most famous and studied of all, United States, have suffered the internal bloodletting, strife, hatred and self-destruction of the infamy of brother against brother. The most famous lands of the Bible are not any exception. Rome and the Roman Empire was in so many ways a construction of civil was until the internal retribution had settled by the time of Christ. The glorious history of Greece, so important not only to the Biblical story and ultimately the seedbed of Western civilization is a story of centuries of permanent political division and depressingly endless civil war. Unity was not achieved until the 330's B.C. and then only by the forcible actions of young Alexander of Macedon.

Endlessly we might observe a historical and current parade of internal strife in nations, ethnicities, tribes and families (a subject to itself), but for our purposes may we not say "Yes, but what about the Jews?" God's Chosen nation was a tiny, almost miniscule, enclave on the shores of the eastern Mediterranean. Even their enemies, whose numbers remain legion, would admit that they have suffered through an unbroken tradition of endless persecution, hatred, genocidal fanaticism and sheer Satanic venom probably unmatched in pure suffering by any people in history. The Jews, Hebrews, Israelites, or by whatever of the many names they were known were sui generis, outcasts morally, religiously, culturally and politically wherever and whenever they lived. The logical presumption we might make is that such worldly opposition brought them together, solidified familial, historical and cultural bonds among them. Such a presumption would be incorrect in the extreme.

The Old Testament history of the Jews was one of disunity among the original twelve tribes to where they finally divided into two nations, Israel and Judah. Israel's final curtain as an independent nation fell in 722 B.C., Judah was subject to foreign captivity and but a handful, the famous "remnant" of the descendants of Abraham finally returned to Judah in the 400's B.C. The remaining Jews were dispersed throughout the world, a world now ruled by Rome politically and the Greeks culturally. These were the children of the Jewish dispersion, the "Diaspora" and they were scattered away from their original Palestinian home. They, of course, remained Jews ethnically but became increasingly acclimated culturally to the dominant Greek, i.e. Hellenistic, culture that had come to dominate so much of antiquity. Their ethnic kinsman, the Palestinian Jews, remained in their ancient homeland of Judea and developed separately from the Hellenistic Jews. Except for language these Jews remained largely untouched by Hellenistic Jews as they developed along a different path.

Still, they were all Jews, and many, if not most, remained faithful to the Law of Moses until that day of Pentecost in circa 30 AD where thousands, be they Palestinian or Hellenistic, became Christians. Unfortunately, though, this great fact did not entirely eliminate another fact, this one more unfortunate, as described by the great writer Luke, himself not a Jew but a Gentile:

> "And in those days when the number of the disciples was multiplied there arose a murmuring of the Grecians against the Hebrews, because their orders were neglected in the daily ministrations."

Were the Hellenistic widows being neglected in the daily benevolence of food distribution? Possibly, perhaps even probably, but the Church leaders, the twelve apostles, were more interested in solving the problem, which must have been extant, rather than assessing blame. Wisely these men knew that their work commissioned by Christ Himself was spreading the truth, rather than "... serving tables." Wisely they selected seven men, all Hellenistic Jews but more importantly, to oversee this work. They were Philip, Prochorus, Nicanor, Timon, Parmenas, Nicholas and Stephen, the latter distinguished as "a man full of faith and of the Holy Spirit." With Stephen begins a world and eternally impacting saga that is bound at one end by vitriolic hatred and the other by a peace incapable of being understood, much less explained.

Of all mortal men and women from the Bible and from recorded history Stephen is the individual whose life and death accomplished so much and about whom we know so little. A few moments in his life and his character are briefly but brilliantly described, his character partially but eloquently revealed and his death and martyrdom so inspiring that to the believer Stephen is forever a role model. His likely short life was a meteor or a comet which speeds across the dark horizon, illuminating however briefly in life but forever in eternity, the love he had for mankind and for God. Through the maddened tumult of his life's finale and the hatred which he ignited among the enemies of Christ his character and conduce was the very essence of the peace of which the apostle spoke.

The seven men chosen by the apostles for the always important task of ministering to the widows, and all were like Stephen, Hellenistic Jews. The work was time consuming, at times likely arduous with physical labor and called for both the strength of youth and the maturity of experience. The apostles chose well, and the first name listed in their selection was Stephen. Certainly he would not have been selected for such important duty if his character was lacking in concern for fellow Christians, not always a given factor. As important as this was (and remains) it is not the most salient fact about Stephen.

"Full of faith and the Holy Spirit" was Stephen as described by the great chronicler Luke. A complete definition of the entirety of that phrases' meaning is beyond our chartered knowledge, but Stephen was "full," a complete man, a complete disciple in so many ways. Among the most obvious were the gifts of speaking, courage and unfaltering dedication. Though the apostles Stephen was anointed by God with the gift of performing miracles, i.e. "... signs and wonders among the people." Those who profited from his faith and wonders loved Stephen, but soon certain Jewish sects, of which there had become an incalculable number, but specifically the Alexandrians, the Libertines and the Cyrenius "disputed" him. Not being able to refute either his record or his logic they "suborned" men, i.e. paid witnesses, to level the accusation that:

> "We have heard him speak blasphemous words against Moses and against God."

To the Christian, these lies and the developing scene sound hauntingly and horrifyingly familiar. To top off this devil's banquet of lying accusations they had the audacity to repeat the charge made against the son of God:

> "We have heard him say that this Jesus of Nazareth shall destroy this place, and shall change the customs which Moses delivered us."

It was soon that Stephen was led to the Sanhedrin Council to presumably answer "charges" just as on that black night years earlier Jesus was dragged before the same council to supposedly answer charges. So there sat Stephen, likely bound with chains and/or shackles, and his simple presence and demeanor gave rise to one of the most remarkable observations of history:

> "All that saw him in the council, looking steadfastly on him, saw his face as it had been the face of an angel."

Neither this author nor his readers has knowingly seen the face of an angel so the internal vision which we all possess must imagine the picture. Likely for those who believe they were viewing Stephen in his heavenly countenance. As a final note to this dramatic and beautiful tableau no such description is made scripturally for any other mortal.

So here we are again, with much of the same dark cast that directed Christ to the cross at Calvary. Caiaphas, the high priest, as corrupt, hate filled and with a heart and soul of vileness directed Stephen to answer the charges with the simple question of "Are these things so?" The clash of this angel of light and peace with the poisonous hatred of this spawn of Satan, Caiaphas, is the prelude to one of the great New Testament sermons where Stephen, surely knowing that he was about to die spoke fearlessly and eloquently of God's plan for the redemption of all mankind. Stephen with faith, aplomb, an undoubted great speaking ability and endless courage addressed an audience, in identity and leadership much the same as that which had condemned Christ. Without faltering he gave a magnificent recitation of God's relationship and plans for humanity, from creation through Moses, the Law, Israel's history and ultimately now salvation offered to Jews and shockingly to Gentiles. The anger, terror and rage which Stephen engendered from his audience and his judges after Stphen bombarded them with this truth can only be imagined:

> "Which of the prophets have not your fathers persecuted? and they have slain them which

> showed before of the coming of the Just One; of whom ye have been now the betrayers and murderers."

Stephen had pierced them to their hearts and so enraged were they that literally they became almost as rabid animals as "... they gnashed on him with their teeth." With Christ they followed a sham legal process to its apparent conclusion on Calvary, but with Stephen their blind, puerile hatred denied him even the further semblance of law.

The tripwire between legal process and mob violence, as thin and tenuous as it was, had now been snapped. The earthly life's tenure of Stephen was now to be measured in but a few minutes. No legal process remained, no formal pronouncements from the Sanhedrin judiciary and certainly not the stamp of the Roman governor's approval. In its place was mob vengeance, more violent and animalistic than any of which the sordid imagination of Hollywood producers and filmmakers could conjure. Jerusalem itself, the holy city, the City of David, could not be putrefied with the blood of a "criminal" as vile as Stephen, and as with the Son of God was dragged past the city gates to be put to death. Not crucifixion this time, though, but rather stoning, itself an execution method of vivid brutality. The condemned was set apart, and as many executioners as could be procured joined in pelting the condemned with stones. Now, but a few, a very few minutes of terrestrial Ife remained to Stephen, the man always known as the first Christian martyr. Stephen wit as true a Spirit of Christ as this life has ever seen resisted not, and doubtless was the calmest, the most peaceful, man present. Luke, with his customary precision and eloquence recorded that:

> "(Stephen), being full of the Holy Spirit, looked up stedfastly into Heaven, and saw the glory of God, and Jesus standing on the right hand of God."

The text of the New Testament records that only three men "looked into Heaven," two being apostles, but the first to do so was Stephen.

The final earthly words of Stephen are hauntingly and suggestively familiar:

> "And they stoned Stephen, calling upon God, and saying, Lord Jesus, receive my spirit."

The coda, the concluding benediction to a short but breathtakingly spectacular life was given by Stephen himself:

> "And he kneeled down, and cried with a loud voice,
> Lord, lay not this sin to their charges.
> And when he said this he fell asleep."

Two millennia hence echoes from Calvary's Cross utter still when we ponder Stephen's benedictory words, an echo of Christ's "Father, forgive them for they know not what they do."

The direct blazing light of illumination which was the life of Stephen had fallen dark. Certainly his martyrdom is remembered with reverent honor. His dedication, natural abilities and talents, faith and courage are themselves ever-bright stars in the Christian firmament. Let us not forget, though, that we think and ponder peace. Stephen undoubtedly was a man of notable kindness evidenced by his assignment of a special responsibility to take care of the Church's widows. Our brief glimpse into his life, though, strikingly, is one of tumult, violence, brutality and hatred, conditions and qualities which are the opposite of peace. Certainly Stephen was given the ultimate treasure of peace, the eternal peace of Heaven with God, but where do we find peace in his life and influence upon others? If the final scenes of Stephen's life were peaceful it is a peace that is hard to understand, at least so in its first consideration. Why is Stephen, as admirable and great a man as he was, still remembered, cherished and venerated by serious Christians who know only his short story recorded in the Book of Acts? Everything about Stephen to both Christians and even fair-minded non-Christians radiates goodness, but his life reached its terminus quickly at a doubtless early age. The greatest writer yet in the English language, William Shakespeare, attributed to a decidedly non-believing Marc Antony these spoken words at a funeral oration in "Julius Caesar:"

> "The evil that men do lives after them: The good
> is oft interred with their bones."

Shakespeare, often as wise as he was gifted, was really having Antony speak sardonically, for in the content of the play and of history he had no intention of letting the "good" of Julius Caesar lie fallow.

We leave it to good historians to discuss and dissect the "good" of Caesar, but of Stephen we observe that as good and pure as was his life his influence in death has proven even greater, for which but little time was required for such to be seen.

The story of Stephen's life is a tale told of the very early days of the Church when the institution, while not geographically exclusive, was still overwhelmingly centered in Jerusalem and by ethnicity exclusively Jewish. The ruling Jewish hierarchical establishment had tasted blood in its persecution and the death of Stephen. They found the taste not just palatable but delightful, and they wanted even more. Their enemy, the followers of the upstart Galilean rabbi, had made an easy target. The mass of them, since the Church's founding had been centered in Jerusalem, and they were easy and convenient targets for imprisonment or even death. Lest they suffer persecution and in the extreme the fate of Stephen their most obvious recourse was to leave Jerusalem and as Luke noted:

> "At that time there was a great persecution against the church which was at Jerusalem; and they were scattered abroad throughout the regions of Judea and Samaria, except the apostles."

Stephen's life and martyrdom had led directly to the desperation, yet another Jewish "Diaspora," and now the persecutors had many fronts on which to wage their hatred and war upon Christ. Neither for the first nor the last time did the sworn enemies of God, Christ and the Truth prematurely celebrate a victory that was actually one of the most devastating blows that Satan and his minions would ever suffer.

To the Jewish politico-religious establishment Jesus of Nazareth was anathema, a man who had introduced into the nation's heart the disease of what would soon be known as Christianity. They crucified Him and quickly dispatched the man who among His early day followers had proven to be the most dedicated, eloquent and magnetic. Their enemy, the no-account Christians were no longer a hard knot of rebellion in the geographic heart and soul of Judean, which was Jerusalem itself. How they began to scatter to the four winds, to the rest of

Judea, to Syria, the numerous provinces of Asia Minor (northern Turkey), the Mediterranean islands, to the ancient, storied and glorious cities of Greece, to neighboring Syria, so many other locales and ultimately to Rome itself, the extant center of the ancient world. Now, their enemy was scattered everywhere, all directly traceable to the martyrdom of a brilliant and beautiful man, a man who died with the face of an angel.

Would the high priest Caiaphas, his cohorts in the Sanhedrin and their many and various fanatical adherents be up to the challenge. One young man was certainly eager to try. Strangely in the full detailed account of the "trial" and murder of Stephen only one man is mentioned by name, and that at the story's end in a seeming afterthought. When Stephen's executioners had dragged him outside the city and in preparation to do their killing as thoroughly as possible "... they laid down their clothes (likely the outer garment worn by Jews) at a young man's feet, whose name was Saul." Likely young Saul, a Jew's Jew and fanatically devoted to his perception of the Law, was for whatever reason(s) too weak and/or frail physically to personally take part in the brutal execution. He was a young man totally and ferociously consumed with zeal, zeal for the Law of Moses, for Judaism and with hatred of Jesus Christ and his followers. One sentence alone gives us pause and understanding of the zealotry and hatred which was consuming Saul:

> "And Saul, yet breathing out threatenings and slaughter against the disciples of the Lord, went unto the high priest."

Young Saul asked of old high priest Caiaphas letters of commission giving him the authority to travel northward to Damascus, the capital of Syria and "... if he found any of this way (i.e. Christ), whether they were men or women, he might bring them bound into Jerusalem." Caiaphas acceded to Saul's petition, and off went Saul and his companions on the road to Damascus. This young man, the proverbial "fair-haired boy" of the Jewish religious establishment journeyed carrying many things. Saul was brilliant, almost frightfully "smart," analytical, totally committed in his beliefs to the righteousness, the exclusive truth and righteousness of the Jewish religion, and a man of great courage. With him, then, traveled brilliance, knowledge, approval and authority from the high and mighty, self-confidence, self-assurance and an overriding certainty of the truth and justice of his opinions. Saul also carried an immense quantity of another quality, and that was hatred. Like all fanatics, religious, political, cultural, etc., those that disagreed with him were not to be convinced otherwise but rather destroyed, or plainly put, killed. What's more he had his holy writ, letters from the high priest and the Sanhedrin, and Saul was not both the accuser, the enforcer, and in a peculiarly modern crime term the hitman of the Jewish hierarchy. His hatred, not just for Christ and Christians, but to any opposition to his carefully determined beliefs and "truths" excited in him a white-hot intensity. He walked in pure hatred.

Those steps, though, suddenly came to a halt when on the Damascus road a bright light from Heaven shined about him and him alone. In a heap he crumbled to the earth and heard the Heavenly voice of "Saul, Saul, why persecutes thou me?" Saul, accustomed to full control, was now groveling in the gravel and dirt of the road when with a sardonic tone the Master spoke:

> "It is hard for thee to kick against the pricks."

"Pricks" were goads utilized to herd livestock, and Saul now found himself literally thrown onto the earth, now without sight and speechless. For the moment at least his hatred was entirely secondary, and his emotional focus was fear. Now he was led by the hand as a child into Damascus, totally helpless, bewildered, fearful and without food, water and eyesight for three days. Saul was more accustomed to discomforting others and injecting into innocent persons fear and terror, but now one of those persons was coming to him, a man with the truth that would upend Saul's life and redirect the course of the history of the church founded by Christ Himself. His name was Ananias and with justifiable fear and apprehension he had received God's message and go to Saul. He approached the still blind Saul as a fellow Jew, and Saul accepted Ananias's teaching immediately, was baptized as a Christian and regained his eyesight.

Saul of Tarsus, headstrong, brilliant, intolerant, and stuffed to overflowing with hatred had passed from darkness to Light, and from hatred to peace, yet a peace of such fabric that he could never have so envisioned. For the time being, though, Saul tasted little of the fruits of peace. Immediately he began worshiping with the other Christians in Damascus, but it is easy to imagine the suspicion which his fellow Christians held inasmuch as the Church's most notorious persecutor was now sitting among them. For the moment (a very long moment, i.e. the remainder of his life) he had now become to his fellow committed Jews that most despicable of all creatures, a traitor. His life was in danger to such an extent that his new Christian brothers secreted him and scrumptiously let him down from the Damascus city walls to save him from the wrath of his one-time cohorts, who "... watched day and night to kill him." Saul had passed from spiritual darkness to spiritual light, but still he lived and walked in the shadow of hatred and would do so the remainder of his days.

Having safely escaped from certain death in Damascus he returned to Jerusalem, his starting point. A tried-and-true phrase of shopworn cliché is that someone is a changed man. We indulge in its application since at no time in the world's history has it been more applicable than with Saul. He now joined himself with the twelve apostles, Peter, James, John and the others, but the meeting was hardly a reunion of brothers who were rhapsodic in their camaraderie. For "... they were all afraid of him and believed not that he was a disciple." And why, based upon his proven character and history, should they have felt differently? He was a man often having proven the deepest hatred for the Son of God and His followers, of whom these men were the specifically chosen dozen. It was the great leader Barnabas, one of the scriptures most unsung and underrated men, and who stepped forth and vouched for Saul's character and "... how he had preached boldly at Damascus in the name of Jesus." Of course, they accepted this highly educated Hellenistic Jew and these men, most of whom were sons of Galilee, would be not the twelve, but the thirteen apostles. Not by Saul's own will, the vote of the apostles or by Barnabas but by the words of Christ who had told Ananias of His desire:

> "(Saul) is a chosen vessel unto Me, to bear my name before the Gentiles, and kings, and the children of Israel.
>
> For I will show him how great things he must suffer for My name's sake."

Outwardly Saul would experience little or no peace in this world. So hated would he and his teachings of Christ be he recognized that to many he would become the "offscouring of all things," a somewhat more archaic version of the "scum of the earth." Physically his life would be harshly brutal, and untold cruelties he would suffer from the natural elements and the hatred of men, men who had always hated Christ. But he would glory in it all, this strange man from Tarsus, and self-proclaim that he was a "fool for Christ." From being a brilliant boiling cauldron for the Son of God Saul was now transformed into a glowing, radiating beacon of life. The personality remained. His self-assured brilliance, likely not an easy or pleasant quality, had to be endured by his colleagues and cohorts, but that hatred been replaced by peace?

To this point our chapter has given far more focus to hatred than to peace, and it is logical for a sincere observer to inquire whether hatred, a despicable quality to be sure, can morph and evolve into peace in the context of the same person. As the world views and defines "peace" Saul's life was one of history's greatest unmitigated disasters. The New Testament itself is largely a story of Saul's travels and travails, and in the latter portion of his life he aptly described it:

> "In prisons ...frequent, in deaths aft.
>
> Thrice was I beaten with rods, once was I stoned, thrice I suffered shipwrecks, a night and a day I have been in the deep.
>
> In journeyings often, in perils of water, in perils of robbers, in perils of mine own countrymen,

> in perils by the heathen, in perils in the city, in
> perils in the wilderness, in perils in the sea
> in perils among false brethren.
>
> In weariness and painfulness, in watchings often,
> in hunger and thirst, in fastings often, in cold and
> nakedness."

Admittedly, the average person may read the apostle Paul's (Saul's Christian title) and find not the description of peace, but rather its antithesis. No one, absolutely no one, would voluntarily assume and live the kind of life which Paul has described unless he received and/or expected a compensation therefor greater than the pain and suffering forced upon him by the enemies of Christ.

It must be remembered that when Saul of Tarsus became a Christian his personality likely changed very little. As the apostle Paul he was the same almost supernaturally (perhaps the "almost" should be struck) driven man he always was. A self-described "Hebrew of the Hebrews," a tireless, indefatigable worker and likely somewhat abrasive and difficult to tolerate even by his closest friends and associates. He was intellectually brilliant, superlatively well read, and could construct and deliver arguments, whether on the offense or defense, as well as any man who ever lived. His physical suffering was of a level and consistency which astonishes even today. Still in spite of all this he is the author of the ever-beautiful phrase of "the peace that passes understanding" when described his and the faithful Christian's treasured gift.

Without any doubt the apostle Paul was a man who could and does yet excite the strongest, dare we say the most rabid of emotions. Later he was the focus of a group of the most rabid of the hardcore of the Jewish establishment whose hatred for the man was so great that once they pledged an oath that they would not eat until they had killed him. Unless two millennia hence these men miraculously live, we may presume that the oath was long ago broken and discarded. Paul was a man who possessed the educational and intellectual credentials to be invited to speak before an august group of Greek philosophers on Mars Hill in the intellectual center of Athens. It is difficult to imagine that such educated and philosophically self-regarding men as these Greek philosophers would ever have deigned to grant such an audience to Galilean fishermen such as Peter, James and John. There in the putative cultural birthplace of Western civilization Paul, inspired by the spirit, acquitted himself beautifully and brilliantly, but still did himself no personal favors by antagonizing these men of academic standing and presumed brilliance.

It remained, though, that Paul's harshest even most ferocious of enemies remained his fellow Jews, men to whom Paul stood as the vilest of heretics and traitors. Literally, he was pursued across boundaries and borders, into large cities, small towns and rural sectors by ardent, fanatical men who hungered for his death. Finally he was taken in the City of David, Jerusalem, the capital of Judea, and the long trail of his life which led to abuse, imprisonment and death began in earnest. Through it all, though, and from a Roman dungeon in the final days of life still was Paul able to proclaim:

> "I know how both to be abased, and I know how to abound: every where and in all things I am instructed both to be full and to be hungry, both to abound and to suffer need."

All those peril and persecutions which Saul of Tarsus had been promised at the outset of His walk in the Light and his apostleship came true. Outwardly, both as the fanatically zealous Saul of Tarsus and then the exemplary apostle Paul this man led a life surrounded by violence and hatred, even the latter of which he was most often as a young man, the author.

Young or old, Paul was a firebrand and in his early days the progenitor of death for many faithful Jews, the most historically famous of which is Stephen. As an apostle and a Christian Paul was never the source of hatred and violence, although clearly his writings reflect that his own regretful past was always on his conscience. For many years, though, Paul had suffered persecution and brutal emotional, spiritual and physical hardships. He ended his earthly sojourn while a prisoner of the Romans in Rome itself. It was during the long and repulsive reign (AD 54-68) of the Roman emperor Nero Claudius Caesar Augustus Germanicus (a/k/a Nero) that early one morning in circa AD 65 Paul, now aged and infirm, was taken from a cell and led to an execution block where a burly Roman legionary severed his head from his body. Being a Roman citizen Paul was spared the disgrace and ignominy of crucifixion, but to the Romans he was still dead. To God, Christ and Paul himself, though, and in his Paul's own phraseology as quick as a "twinkle in the eye" he was transformed into the real life of eternity with Christ. Truly, he was and so remains in the glorious presence and Light of the Prince of Peace.

About thirty-five years, more than a single generation, had now passed since the death, burial and resurrection of Jesus Christ. His Church had been established and the wisdom of His choice of the first twelve apostles and then Paul had been demonstrated time and again. His Church and His teachings were being spread throughout the world, and its growth from a tiny knot of Jewish disciples in Jerusalem to locales that dotted the maps of Asia, Europe and Africa had been astounding. Jesus of Nazareth's birth had been announced by that angelic declaration of "peace on earth, good will towards men" and so it was true. Still, though, it exacerbated hatreds as we have witnessed in the lives of two men, Stephen and Paul.

The earthly story which had begun its course approximately thirty years before in a grim, but beautiful scene, outside Jerusalem had run its course and had terminated with the violent death of Paul in Rome. The story was of two men, Stephen and Paul (nee Saul) who had clearly in definite stances on opposite sides of a sharply drawn line. We have neither Biblical nor secular evidence that the two men had ever met or knew each other, although each was probably well aware of the other's public reputation. The line between them was not misunderstanding, misapprehension or any of the softer terms of the modern therapeutic culture. Rather it was that line which the great nineteenth century Russian novelist Dostoevsky remarked was the true, exacting line. It was the line between good and evil which runs through every human heart. On that day circa AD 35 Stephen, even in death was literally forgiving and angelic as he waited to fall into the arms of Christ. While his body was being pummeled and destroyed his heart and soul were at peace. Saul, still consumed with hatred for this new heretical Christian sect, and if wholesale murder was needed so it shall be. Possessed of unparalleled intellect and seemingly unstoppable determination, he was hurled forward by hatred until that fateful day on the road to Damascus. Confronted by the voice and challenge of the Son of God Himself Saul turned the direction of his life and the virulent hatred within him was turned from the disciples of Christ to its proper target, Satan.

The stories of Stephen and Paul have been told and retold, and hopefully so they shall ever be until the end of terrestrial time. The hatred which had consumed and driven Paul forward while young was history, and the apostle, this man of all people, could legitimately write later that he possessed the peace that passes understanding. In his abbreviated Biblical appearance Stephen possessed such peace from beginning to end. Undoubtedly throughout his splendid but rough and tough apostolic days Paul thought of Stephen often, and how that he as Saul had been one of the prime movers in Stephen's stoning. With wonderful splendor the Christian may contemplate the Heavenly bond of these two extraordinary men. There hatred will be unknown, and all live in the Light of the Prince of Peace.

CHAPTER NINE

THE POST BIBLICAL CHURCH

The terrestrial stage of the Great Story, the redemption of humanity by man, saw the earthly departure of Jesus Christ by His ascension to Heaven circa AD 30. The four gospels are His personal story, a kind of multi-authored biography that ends with not the death of the protagonist but rather the proclamation of eternal life for all mankind. The four gospels, not yet written, would be followed by an additional twenty-three books penned by His closest followers, men who in almost every instance had been personally well acquainted with the Savior. With but one exception, the Acts of the Apostles, meticulously and beautifully written by the Greek physician, all these books were written by apostles, by men wo had personally known and walked with Christ. This included the most prolific writer, the apostle Paul, the apostle "born out of due season" who had met Christ on the road to Damascus as well as undoubtedly seeing Him face to face as he was being instructed in his apostolic role. These men did not cease to be frail humans, though they were endowed by their Creator with the Holy Spirit and possessed authority and influence that no man ever since has shared. These were the men of whom the scriptures proclaimed were the "foundation of the Church, Jesus Christ being the chief cornerstone." For three years they had walked with Him, listened to His teachings and with their own eyes had witnessed the many miraculous signs and wonders with which He still stuns humanity. The prestige and reputation of these men was great, although by no means did all believe that their lives were inviolate with perfection or their teachings incontrovertible. They had fierce opposition without and at times within the Church, and little by little, one by one, their lives ended in violence. It began with James, the son of Zebedee, one of the Master's inner circle who was murdered by King Herod Agrippa I. Others followed, eventually even the two most famous, the apostles Peter and Paul, who were executed by the Romans. Historical tradition is that all the apostles save one, the beloved John, died violent deaths. John, who penned the final book of the New Testament, Revelation in the AD 90's likely died of natural causes soon thereafter where he was exiled a prisoner on the Isle of Patmos.

For lack of a better term the Church which Christ Himself founded was the apostolic Church, an increasingly polyglot body of believers whose great focus of unity was Jesus Christ (who yet remains the sole unitizing power). Beginning as an exclusively Jewish organization its geographic reach began to expand enormously and soon the Gentile world came into the fold to the point that by the end of the first century their numbers began to predominate. It was wonderful to still have the direct personal influence of the apostles on Christians and church matters, but it was not a guarantor of purity and tranquility. The New Testament is rife with stories of internal church strife, divisions, sectarianism and much self-promotion, although in general the Church remained true to the simple spirit and teachings of Christ, as exemplified by the apostles in their lives and words. Their influence remained great, although slowly with the passage of time and the diminution of theirs numbers it began to wane. Even in the first century false teachers began to arise, false teaching that was anathema to the depth and purity of Christ.

For a thorough history and detailed account of the menace of false doctrine the New Testament itself is naturally the revealed source. Briefly, though we note two great false ideas that arose during the "childhood" of the early Church and were quite instrumental in deleterious influence. The first and by far the easier to explain is that which emanated from the so-called Judaizing Christians. The Jews, of course, had carried the lineage of the Savior and had long been God's Chosen, given their special and esteemed Law of Moses. While these Jews (by ethnicity) accepted Christ and as Gentiles began to enter the Church, they taught that to be really acceptable to God a Gentile Christian must also be circumcised and practice the rites and rituals of Judaism. Eventually time, the stubbornness and the recalcitrance of the Jews in large degree solved this apostasy inasmuch as Jews who followed Christ became numerically diminished to the vanishing point. Still, even with the apostolic presence in the early Church it was a major obstacle, especially to Paul, the chosen apostle to the Gentiles.

The second great problematic issue to the early Church was one that in various forms and guises is still a potent force in the twenty-first century. It went by the title "Gnosticism." It is a term from the Greek language, "gnosis" meaning knowledge and was and is incapable of a dictionary definition in a single phrase or sentence. Collectively it was a strange phantasmic collaboration of religious or more popularly "spiritual" beliefs that emphasized a person's own knowledge over orthodox and simple religious teachings. Its variations are as numbered as the stars of the sky, and its followers continue to radiate "new" ideas and philosophies that shine brightly in the firmament of their eyes. Gnosticism, the shape, form, effects and influence ebbed and flowed in the early years of the Church, and in various intellectual forms it yet exerts an influence and presence on Christianity. The Judaizing teachers of the early Church attempted at times successfully, to pull the Church into the nasty quagmire of legalism, a deleterious influence which lives still; however, Gnosticism, which in its practice essentially asserted human feeling above the simple teachings of the Good Shepherd, has proven even more harmful to the Church.

Nevertheless from the distance of two millennia we may observe and remark that the early Church founded by Christ and nourished by His apostles was, at the conclusion of the first century, a remarkable success story. Begun as a knot of Galilean fishermen and other Jews whose birth and background was obscure by the work of these apostles and their associates and the guidance of God it had by 100 AD developed into a widespread phenomenon. While still maintaining a presence in Judea it had spread south to Ethiopia, eastward to Asia Minor (now Turkey), Persia and perhaps as far as India. Northward and westward into the storied lands of classical civilization, Greece and Rome, it had spread in spite of efforts of its persecutors to destroy it. From the New Testament we know little or nothing of its size, membership and numbers, but obviously they were enough to excite the vicious persecution, albeit sporadic, of the Roman powers. With the blessings of God and of Christ it was truly the "bride of Christ," a beautiful bride but still one with Flaws that the scriptures took no effort to hide. Jealousy, backbiting, power struggles, self-exaltation and just plain worldliness were found in the early Church. Still, though, the faithful Christian was indeed faithful to Christ and for the most part the simplicity and a striving for moral purity were essentials to any description of the Church as the first century closed.

It would not always be so. From the Day of Pentecost in circa AD 30 to the Last Judgment it would have been (and so remains) ludicrous to believe that all would be smooth sailing calm seas and perfection for the disciples of Christ. Towards the end of his remarkable life and career, the apostle Paul wrote his second letter to the church in Thessalonica, a major city in Macedonia. He spoke of the glorious day when Christ would come again, but he also warned his fellow Christians to:

> "Let no man deceive you by any means: for that day (the Second Coming of Christ) shall not come, except there come a falling away first, and that more of sin be revealed, the son of perdition.
>
> Who opposeth and exaltith himself above all that is called God, or that is worshipped; so that he as God sitteth in the temple of God, showing himself that he is God."

Many have believed and taught that Paul is referencing his knowledge of a coming apostasy (a "falling away") that will result in the destruction of the simplicity of the Church founded by Christ and eventually the exaltation of an office and its holder, the Roman papacy, above all other men. Regardless of the full theological meaning of Paul's admitting it should be recognized that the Church began to gradually, very gradually, shed the pure simplicity of its apostolic age of the first century.

Although Biblical source material ceased and secular historical accounts for the AD 100's and 200's are scant we may still make intelligent surmise of the state of the Church during this period. As earlier noted, its growth was widespread and as always with true Christianity deceptively powerful. In the words of the Savior Himself light was now penetrating the repressive darkness in areas and regions that had never known hope. The conduct of Christians in hitherto barbarian lands must have been especially notable, even startling. A new form of man and woman was being seen, one that was not totally consumed with self and self-aggrandizement and who showed (mostly) concern, great care and concern, for his neighbors. He or she was not violent, not totally consumed with worldly gain and riches and who seemed to live not for themselves but also for the good of others. What's more they were not alone for long, and their numbers seemed to be multiplying. Law-abiding, good citizens and subjects, they shone with more than a patina of difference, and difference is noticeable and after exciting of hostility. The mass of people, not just a stray eccentric individual here or there but increasingly larger groups of persons who were living lives beyond their own self-interests and with concerns for others.

These two centuries were a remarkable time for the Church's expansion and growth. The Church certainly was not lacking in leadership, great tinkers and theologians, men such as Clement of Rome, Irenaeus, Clement of Alexandria, Tertullian and Polycarp, himself an associate and student of the apostle John. Their lives and writings are studied yet today, and are especially valuable in providing an understanding of a long period where our knowledge of Church history is scant. The growth, fame and teachings of the early Church were a blessing, but unfortunately as with all good the Prince of this World finds a way to mirror the good with evil. The Church of Jesus Christ had begun as an institution of notoriety and publicity in Jerusalem in the obscure Roman province of Judea, which approached upwards to a thousand miles distance from the great center of Rome. We have seen that from the beginning it was subject to persecution, as witness Stephen, but it was a persecution by the Jewish religious establishment. To the outside Gentile world, especially Rome where most great political decisions were made, it was no more than another Jewish cult religion, of which the Romans had seen plenty. As long as they were relatively quiet the Romans left the Christians alone.

In the early AD 60's the skies began to darken for the Church. It had now expanded into the Gentile world and into Rome itself, which contained a considerable body of Christians. The first great conflagrations of persecution began in the AD mid-60's when the Emperor Nero, drunk with power but increasingly fearful of his own tenuous status put to use the great fire of Rome in AD 64 as an excuse to blame the Christians, whereupon he unleashed on them a persecution still a byword for brutal viciousness. Nero himself was assassinated in 70 AD, but the effeminate tyrant had set in motion a despotic persecution of Christians so harsh and vile that the gentle apostle John later referred to Rome as "... the great whore, drunken with the blood of the saints." Although we moderns are confronted with a paucity of historical records and rarely any mention of numbers it is apparent that even while persecuted as the second century AD marched onward so did the expansion of the religion of the Savior.

Certainly persecution was vicious, but generally it seemed to be localized and subject to interruptions by changes in emperors and local governing officials. Much of the time Rome had many other things on its collective imperial mind, but when it turned its thoughts and gaze upon the Church as the AD 100's progressed it began to find much that was objectionable. For one thing, Rome rested largely on its military prowess, and it found that Christians were reluctant to join its army, an army that required an oath of loyalty to the emperor and a declaration that he himself was a divine god. Such was anathema to the Christians, and this in the eyes of many these strange religious fanatics were disloyal and unpatriotic. This burden of opprobrium and at times violent persecution was being borne by a people who were taught explicitly and implicitly by their Savior and their faith's Founder to always obey civil government and be respectful to its directors unless they conflicted with those of God.

As jolting and baffling as the allegations of disloyalty must have been to the early Christians infinitely more so were the wild and salacious rumors that began to abound that these followers of Jesus were cannibals. Yes, cannibals. The early Christians as shown and directed by the Master weekly partook of Communion, the Lord's Supper or what some would come to call the Eucharist. At the Last Supper with His apostles Jesus had passed around the unleavened bread with His direction to "take and eat, for this is my body" and the cup of wine, His Blood which they were to drink, and His disciples thereafter commemorate. Those antithetical to Christ pounced upon the symbolism and the rumors spread that in secret these strange followers of the Nazarene rabbi were practicing human cannibalism. Most obviously Christ had been speaking symbolically and spiritually, but to those who feared and loathed this new religion they had found yet another "reason" for its persecution.

Still the Church spread and grew, but the simplicity of the first century gradually began to succumb to organization and bureaucracy. The simple structure of the early Church began to be cluttered by organization, the creation and appointment of offices unfound in the scriptures and the elevation of certain men above others. While the early New Testament epistles had ordained a simple congregational governing body of elders, or bishops, shepherds, presbyters, one man in certain churches began to assume a greater role and governing power over others. Not only that but congregations of disciples gradually began to shift their allegiance to one man, a bishop, who rules over many churches. The simplicity of God, the beauty and strength of the Church founded by Christ Himself began to stray into a realm where it began to resemble civil government.

Eventually a consensus among those who held power in the Church coalesced around the concept that the Church must have one leader, one bishop above all others, an actual vicar of God who would rule on earth. He would be the head of the Church, its father, its papacy and most commonly referenced as the "pope." Traditional Roman Catholicism attributes to a simple unlettered Galilean fishermen, the apostle Simon Peter, its honor as the first pope. While Catholicism recognizes that Peter had authority among all others never so did Christ or any of the scriptures. Certainly, Peter himself would have been aghast at the very thought. Nonetheless at some point in the AD 100's, 200's, or 300's the growing power and prestige of the Bishop of Rome was recognized and conceded.

The sincere reader should be spared any extended history of what came with the papacy and the more highly organized and structural church edifice. Suffice it to say that in time such offices as cardinals, bishops, various prelates and increasing bureaucracy began to fill continually created posts until the church itself became a hive of bureaucracy. Organization, lines of responsibility, hierarchical responsibilities gradually and often roughly pushed themselves to the fore. The church's membership undoubtedly grew, but likewise did its initial drift away from the simplicity of Christ's founding grow in proportion. Power and organization, the former legitimately granted only to Christ and the latter rarely if even mentioned by Him became paramount in the Church. Surely many true sincere Christians remained who did their best to serve the Savior, but in AD 312 an event of huge, but often misstated and misunderstood consequences stamped a deep imprint upon the pages of secular and religious history.

The Roman emperor Constantine, a warrior/emperor (as were many in the offices) officially recognized the legality of Christianity and immediately shifted the religious status from that of a persecuted minority to a group favored by the state. Persecution ceased, confiscated church properties returned to the Church and Constatine pledged his sword to be in service of Christ. The easing and then the cessation of persecution was a blessing to the followers of God. It was, though, the proverbial two-edged sword. Although Roman history shows radical policy vacillations from the various emperors who followed Constantine the unmistakable trend was an increasing recognition and promotion of Christianity as "the" state religion. Save for the promises of the Savior Himself that nothing could destroy His Church this seemingly could have been the death knell of true Christianity. It was not; however, state recognition meant state influence, state control and the spiritually diluting influence of the state. The civil recognition of Christianity as the "state" religion helped cause the Church to morph into an object that likely was anathema to its founder, the Son of God who was also a simple Galilean carpenter.

Descent Into Darkness

Officially, Rome at least in western Europe, fell in AD 476 with the deposing of the final Roman emperor, a young man named Romulus Augustulus. The Rome of the Caesars had reached its point of cessation, but its historical and religious legacies were enormous. We have concerned ourselves only with the latter, and assert with reasonable cogency that in this field Rome's greatest legacy has been the Roman Catholic Church, which was now so titled and the power of which in all Europe and other continents had spread and deepened into the body politic and the consciences of so many men and women. This shall not be taken as a screed or diatribe against the Roman Catholic Church but rather a brief, at times simplistic, history of a period which lasted perhaps an entire millennium.

The term "Dark Ages" has been variously defined, limited and expanded, but often is employed to denote that period of time from the "official" fall of Rome in 476 to perhaps the eighth or ninth centuries. Formal learning had weakened, most were illiterate, and the Roman church itself was the main repository for most learning and education, and for this it is to be respected. Unfortunately, though, as central governments weakened to the point often of non-existence in southern, western and northern Europe especially, the Roman Church began to assume many functions not just of religion but of state authority. This is a death knell for pure religion, especially Christianity, as state and church began to synchronize into one all-powerful entity. Churchmen, often the only literate persons available, controlled not only the church but state authority as well. Most fearful and insidious, though, is that church officials began to assume the sole right of thinking and interpreting God's will to others. Increasingly the Roman Church became a power, even secularly at times, greater than the old Roman Empire. It provided not so much spiritual guidance but rather rigid life direction and was of greater succor to those who provided it funding for an increasingly top-heavy organization. This is neither to ignore nor dismiss a recognition that at all times undoubtedly there existed many humble souls who sought only to follow the Light of Christ. The government of Catholicism, though, became more complex, more removed from the people and in many ways likely more removed from God and the simplicity of the early Church.

As the centuries followed one upon the other in these so-called Middle Ages the Church government became so powerful that its head, the papacy, could and would dictate the identity, and governing principles of various rulers. In peril of not just his soul but his office, a king had to consider the desires and policies of a pope whose temporal reach was greater than the King's own powers. It was a long way from Christ's proclamation that "My kingdom is not of this world." As the years, the decades and the centuries elapsed the Church of Rome plunged ever deeper into the abyss. The supposed "bride" of Christ had become historically and religiously degenerate. What those in ecclesiastical power doubtlessly viewed as a great asset was in reality perhaps its greatest stumbling block. It was a body that neither permitted, encouraged nor even brooked opposition, politically or theologically.

We expose no outlying or heretical opinion when we not only aver but also emphatically state that the Roman Church became monstrously, hideously corrupt. Historians, church officials and committed Catholics have decided opinions that the Church had become repulsively corrupt, a corruption, depending upon the individual scholar, that reached its nadir in the period from 1200-1500. Ecclesiastical law became almost

Satanically severe, and dissenters were grist for the active mills of capital punishment.

Dissent, even mild disagreement would be ruthlessly suppressed. It was a period in the history of Europe, the region which had become the heart of Christendom. Lands in which the Church's power was most deeply riveted into the body politic, such as Spain, which developed the infamous Inquisition to crush all alleged "heresy" were particularly bad. The morality of much of the clergy, from the local priests, bishops and cardinals up to and especially including the papacy had become grotesque in its perfidy. The sexual morality of a class that had determined to be known as celibate had become a monstrosity from hell. Church prostitution for which much of the clergy openly availed itself was common. Of a certainty it must be recognized that not all this was by any means universal, and undoubtedly honest and sincere clergymen could be seen. Yet it was not in the sins of the flesh alone, or perhaps even predominately that the apostasy of the church was most noted. An institution as large and widespread as the late Medieval Roman Catholic Church required immense amounts of money for its operations and its self-glorification.

Towards the end of the Middle Ages the papacy and his Roman Church developed a doctrine and a practice that still excites our awe, wonder and disgust. Historically it has become infamous by the phrase the "selling of indulgences." The Church of Rome, already the wealthiest institution in the world, was always grasping for money. Not the simple solicitation of donations and alms giving taught by Christ and His apostles in the early church. The Roman Catholic Church of the late Middle Ages was already wealthy, but like many persons and institutes it reached for more. The pontiffs and prelates had found their gold mine, their earthly treasure, by themselves marketing a heavenly treasure in a practice known as the "selling of indulgences." All men and women are sinners, then, now and as long as this terrestrial world exists, a rare point on which essentially all serious-minded individuals agree. What does one do, say, think, pray, etc., that can eliminate the effects of sin upon life and escape eternal punishment, so justly earned. By the 1300's Catholicism began to develop the means by which its members could effectively mitigate, if not eliminate purchase of an "indulgence" from the Church, wherein the Church would absolve, i.e. effectively forgive the sins of the purchaser. The more one paid the more one's sins would be forgiven. Of course, the entire concept shoves aside the theological foundation that God alone forgives sins. Perhaps it is not too cynical to aver that the Church may have been more beholden to the idea of increasing its own wealth and that of the papacy, priesthood and assorted prelates, with forgiveness and eternal reward being secondary. The entire concept was cynicism, hypocrisy and money grabbing in the guise of religion, concepts with which humanity has never been without acquaintance. The Church, though, was not lacking in persons of religious sincerity, who were adamantly opposed to the throbbing, pulsating mass of corruption the Roman Church had become. Some even held church offices and were increasingly emboldened to speak out. Especially noteworthy was a brilliant youthful priest from Wittenberg, Germany. His name was Martin Luther.

CHAPTER TEN

CONFLICT AND REFORMATION

Martin Luther, who was born into a prosperous family in Eisleben, Germany in 1483, was fated to become one of the most influential figures in religious history and a man of mighty influence in literally shaping and redirecting the course of Western Civilization. His father, a prosperous owner of copper mines, was a local official of some political influence and provided well for Luther, his mother and siblings. His desire was for Martin to become a lawyer, and to that course of study Martin applied himself but like many legal aspirants before and since found it was not to his liking and dropped out. In spite of his disappointed father's fury he redirected his studies to philosophy and the Catholic priesthood. With a brilliant mind, a dedicated work ethic, and sincere Christian beliefs he rose quickly in the atmosphere and environs of German academia, becoming a monk, a Doctor of Theology and a lifetime's association with the University of Wittenberg.

Luther became and yet remains the single most dominant figure in what became known as the Protestant Reformation, but it would be unjust historically and religiously to accord to him the entire salutary honors of this movement. Many other men figure prominently in the Reformation, a large number predating Luther. To them we momentarily grant our attention before returning to Luther and his cataclysmic struggle with the overwhelming and overweening pride of the Roman Catholic Church. By no means does our narrative mean to diminish Luther's historically noteworthy influence but rather we seek to place this remarkable German of many talents within a proper context. He remains the most famous of the Protestant reformers, who like all men were partakers of various human weaknesses. Whether Luther was the most influential is a question for the Almighty Himself.

As we have noted the Roman Catholic Church and what passed for Christianity by the late Middle Ages in a vile and wretched condition. In many places in Europe the Church and the state were two sides of the same coin, dual institutions which were symbiotically supportive one of the other and a great, powerful tent for evil men to exercise almost unlimited powers in the names of God and King. Not only evil, but corrupt men also walked the moral landscape, in these times of ecclesiastical corruption to the point of diseased rottenness. A few other names, most not as bright, illustrious or famous as Martin Luther deserve more than just a passing nod. Each in his own way was hugely influential, an influence that lingers to our days of modernity.

Jan Hus (1368-1415) was a Czech theologian and philosopher and was among the first to peal the alarm bells regarding the ever-deepening corruption of the Roman church. Hus lived and died over a century before Luther and obviously the former never knew of the latter, but the reverse assuredly could not be averred. Hus himself was a Catholic priest, but a priest who increasingly noticed matters of harsh doctrine which he looked upon as askance with the simple teachings of Jesus Christ. Long before Luther, Hus found the practice of the selling of indulgences abhorrent and a mockery of the life and simple teachings of Christ. Among other things that Hus noticed and railed against was the glorification of the centuries long series of wars known yet today as the Crusades. Doubtless there existed some sincerity among the "Christian warriors" who traveled from Europe to the Middle East to battle the Islamic forces which had geographical and political control of the ancient land of Israel, but Hus believed sincerely and correctly that the Crusades were wasteful indulgences of lives and property primarily led by those who sought riches, fame and political/historical notoriety. Rather it was wasteful glorified freebooting totally at odds with Christ's admonition that "he who lives by the sword shall perish by the sword." Certainly, Hus created a stir, a whirlwind of emotions and hateful antipathy within the power centers of the church. For his analysis of events, outspokenness and defiance of the age's power brokers, he suffered the agonies and excruciating pains of being burned at the stake on July 6, 1415. Gone from this world for over six centuries his name and courage still resonate among the knowing. Hus, a man himself both brilliant and courageous, did not appear and operate void of the influence of others, one of whom was an Englishman who predated him by a generation.

John Wycliffe (1328-1384) an English priest, who in many respects, if not the first prominent figure of the Reformation, was the forerunner of the Protestant Reformation. Likely he never even heard the word "Protestant" and instead was himself a Catholic priest for the majority of his adult life. He was though one of the greatest early thinkers in the opposition to long established Catholic doctrines which Wycliffe viewed as heretical to the simple teachings of Jesus Christ. Some of these teachings, embedded deeply in the psyche of the roman Catholic Church included the veneration of saints (a practice from which the church in its financial savvy was able to extract money from its members), icons and their worship, monasteries and the monks who therein abided, the doctrine of Transubstantiation during the Eucharist, and perhaps most dangerously his questioning of the legitimacy of the papacy. In all events in the Catholic hierarchical establishment the supreme power of the papacy had to be sustained. The belief, unspoken though it was, dictated the supreme inviolable power of this one man, the so-called vicar of Christ on earth. It was and remains an office totally estranged from any authority ever granted by the Church's founder, Christ, yet it had become of awe-inspiring power and influence, not just in internal church matters but perhaps even more importantly in the political realm. As courageous and "radical" as were the ideas of Wycliffe and as theologically changing as would be their implementation in the Roman Catholic Church likely the most important religious and practical contribution made by Wycliffe was in the realms of linguistics and literature. John Wycliffe undertook the first serious and extensive translation of the Holy Bible from the ancient classical languages to the everyday vernacular of his fellow Englishmen. In a time of limited literacy it was easy for the Church to maintain a mystery and darkness in which the scriptures were enshrouded. Wycliffe translated a substantial portion of the ecclesiastically approved Latin Vulgate version of the Bible into the commonly spoken English of the people. It was anathema to the Catholic establishment, although several decades later they would face a greater challenge from a far greater English translation of the Bible. The Catholic Church of the late Middle Ages grew and prospered only in the stygian darkness of illiteracy supplemented by the lack of a Bible in the common language of the people. For what Wycliffe believed, taught and presented through his English translation he was a potentially lethal threat to the Roman Church and had to be silenced. His capture and death, however, were not to be at the hands of the Roman church. Throughout his teachings which increasingly questioned the foundational doctrines of the Roman Catholic Church Wycliffe himself remained not only a Catholic but also an actively practicing priest. Whether one applies the overly used word "ironic" the fact is that one day while performing his priestly dues in saying mass Wycliffe suffered a stroke from which he soon expired. When Wycliffe passed, the Roman Catholic Church remained seemingly invincible and inviolate, but its exalted status would soon suffer from far fiercer and more powerful attacks. John Wycliffe was an early, but a key figure in the historical and religious cataclysm which was on the horizon.

Only one decade after the death of Wycliffe another Englishman of religious note was born, a man whose own lifespan was severed in relative youth by the fears and hatred of the Roman Catholic establishment at its work. He was William Tyndale, a man whose lasting influence is arguably greater than that of the other and at times more celebrated reformers. Here in the twenty-first century his influence remains great and growing and likely will never abate so long as the sun and moon continue to shine on this small terrestrial orb. Strangely, perhaps even ironically, this man, William Tyndale (1494-1536) was not really a reformer per se. While he was a rather low-born and low-ranking priest his influence in his professional position likely was relatively minor. Tyndale's world and his forte was language, and truly he could justifiably lay claim to being the greatest linguist of his age. Tyndale, Oxford educated, was proficient in the classical languages of Greek, Hebrew and Latin as well as his own native English, a tongue which in its later stages of maturing. While a young priest he became enraged at the existing church policy of keeping its membership in the dark ignorance of illiteracy. This served existing Church policy well, for a membership that knew not the Word of God, a Word which was shrouded in ancient languages which only a few academics and a handful of the clergy knew. Obviously, the typical English farmer, shopkeeper or laborer knew not Greek or Hebrew and was entirely dependent upon the dictated interpretation of scriptural meaning from a priesthood, a band of clergy that by this time had become honeycombed with immorality and worldly rot. Tyndale, though, was determined and certain that God desired His word to be understood by all races, nationalities and educational levels, and to himself he first commissioned the burden of translating the New Testament from Greek to English. The opposition to such spiritual impudence was a conflagration of rage, from the local priesthood up to the papacy and the various royal figures with whom they prospered in a symbiotic relationship of moral and especially financial corruption. Tyndale, marvelously, some would say Divinely gifted as a linguist and translator began his labor first translating the New Testament into the everyday language of the people. For this he was condemned as a criminal and became known as "God's Outlaw." This man, though, was as bold as he was brilliant and stepped backwards from no opposition. Tyndale's character is more than faintly reminiscent of the apostle Paul.

One vignette from Tyndale's life well illustrates his tenacity, courage, devotion to Truth and his brilliance with words. It has been oft told and with differing words, but we offer a common version. Tyndale was dining with others, including a bishop of the Church who adamantly opposed and condemned Tyndale's labors as a translator, resting secure in the now time-honored belief of the Roman Church that the scriptures did not belong in the hands of ordinary and by definite implication dull, ignorant Christians but rather were to be privately safe-guarded and interpreted by the Catholic clergy alone. To the bishop who haughtily expressed these opinions to Tyndale the latter replied:

> "With my translation of the Bible into English the farm boy behind his plow will know more scripture than you."

Such opinions and his boldness in their expression won Tyndale no applause and instead gave him notoriety and intensified the hatred of the religious establishment for the man. To escape the persecution and personal destruction that awaited him at the hands of England's notorious King Henry VIII, Tyndale fled to the Continent to continue his work. Tyndale had personally incurred Henry's rage by speaking against his notorious divorce from his first wife, Queen Catherine, and subsequent adulterous remarriage to Anne Boleyn. He fled to the Flemish territory of the Roman Catholic Church's Holy Roman Empire and there, having been betrayed by a presumed friend, was apprehended and imprisoned in a castle outside Brussels, Belgium. He remained imprisoned for over one and a half years, continually writing and translating and bypassing all opportunities to save his life by refusing to deny his beliefs. Finally, in the fall of 1536 he was condemned for heresy and strangled to death immediately before being burned at the stake. The Reformation movement continued, though, and its effects were spreading throughout northern, western and central Europe. The favored position of the Roman Catholic's Church in England had but a short period of life remaining. Its fall from its perch of superiority and the creation of the Anglican Church, with the worldly Henry VIII its chief midwife is one of history's most famous stories, but its retelling is beyond the scope of this short work.

Five centuries after his death certainly William Tyndale is remembered yet today, but probably not to the degree and the acclaim his life and work deserve. His was the first translation of the Holy Bible directly from the original languages into English. As referenced earlier he completed the New Testament and had done the majority of the Old at the time of his death. In 1604 the King of England commissioned a new, "authorized" version of the entire Bible into English, a task which was completed in 1611. The translators produced a work with a religious depth and literacy majesty yet unmatched by any book in the English language. It is estimated that the translation is really just an update of Tyndale's work, and that over 80% of its words are Tyndale's. It is inspired in a multiplicity of ways, the greatest literary work in any language, but its English version is the magnum opus of one man, William Tyndale. Over four hundred years later we still know it by its title, the King James Version of the Bible.

The growing Reformation produced other leaders, each of whom were hugely influential in their day and some whose influence remains yet mighty and influential in religious thought and practice Huldrych Zwingli (1484-1531) was the leader of the Reformation in Switzerland, a small but highly influential country in the Alps of Central Europe. Centered in Zurich, Zwingli was a priest, but an accessible clergyman and so beloved that he became known as the People's Priest. Of great importance to Zwingli was a matter that remains of monumental importance to all serious Christians, Holy Communion. By the time of Zwingli the Communion service, the Mass, was recited in Latin, a language unknown to but a few and was of a highly formalistic nature. Zwingli desired its simplification to where it resembled the celebration in that famed upper room on the night before Christ's crucifixion where He with the beautiful simplicity which marked His every word and action showed His sacramental Body and Blood with the apostles. To this beautiful and expressive Lord's Supper Zwingli wished to return.

With only the possible but not the certain exception of Martin Luther the Reformation leader with the greatest and most enduring theological influence was a man from France, John Calvin (1500-1564). To express and define "Calvinist" theology in one or two paragraphs is indeed a fool's errand. Still, though, his following has been so great, these "Calvinists," often a term of derision, have formed a large coterie of Protestantism ever since and in more recent times what is often (again with some measure of derision) called "evangelicalism." In his teachings Calvin emphasized predestination, practical theology, simplicity in worship, salvation by faith and the importance of high moral standards as part of the very essence of Christianity. Calvin's influence remains great in many churches where most of their members may never have heard his name. Generally they are the less prestigious denominations (yes, even many Christian adherents have accorded to themselves various levels of prestige and status). These would include the original Presbyterian churches, the Baptists and various charismatic bodies, whose aggregate numbers far exceed the so named "mainline churches." John Calvin's teaching and influence possibly may be more effective and morally determinative in the lives of more persons than that of Martin Luther.

Still, without dwarfing or in any way diminishing the accomplishments of the great reformers and translators, religiously, historically and culturally any discussion of the Protestant

Reformation should place Martin Luther at its earthly center. During his lifetime and in the centuries since Luther has been accused of so many deplorable qualities. He has been described as overbearing, even a bully, intolerant of others views, racist, bigoted, even a self-promoter; however, it is doubtful that anyone could reasonably accuse him of lacking courage.

By the year 1517 Luther had become well known in Church circles for his somewhat unorthodox theological beliefs. By then he had become an ordained priest and a theological professor at Wittenberg University. Having achieved some notice and fame from the growing debate on the sale of indulgences. On October 31, 1517, he wrote to Bishop Arthur von Brandenburg protesting the sale of indulgences along with an attachment of other theological points of Catholicism which he protested and usually challenged. This document became known as the Ninety-Five Theses which Luther then allegedly nailed to the church door of All Saints Church in Wittenberg. They were points of challenge to extant Catholic doctrine, and if any one day may be proclaimed as the birth of the Protestant Reformation this was it. Many of Luther's theses were directed towards the practice of the Church's selling of indulgences to raise money for ever more ornate and elaborate structures, basilicas, ecclesiastical, etc. Instead of continually extracting money from the very persons who needed it most the Church and each Christian should be engaged in helping the poor. Further, he argued in this document that true Christian repentance was a matter of a person's heart rather than the recitation of rote "confessions" which had been prepared by others.

In point of fact many of Luther's theses were not argumentative nor directly contradictory to the authority of either the church or the papacy but were more in the nature of a reasoned summons for study and discussion of various issues.

Nonetheless the die had been cast, and to the establishment of the Roman Catholic Church Martin Luther had become an incontrovertible enemy, whose influence and, if necessary, his person to be destroyed. He was given one final chance in 1520 to renounce his heresy, and when he refused, was excommunicated in 1521, a status he retained until his death twenty-five years later.

For such a serious man and subject as Martin Luther, his life and influence it is laughable to believe that the brevity of a few page summary of his theological beliefs, religious battles and influence could come close to the justice these topics demand. For our purposes, though, perhaps the greatest of Luther's legacies rests in his well-reasoned and generally scripturally sound reasoning that eternal salvation comes from the grace of God given to the faithful believer. To Luther, and dare we add to Christ Himself, salvation is not formulaic and does not come as some Divine payment for designated "works" dictated by clergy, over-staffed church bureaucracies, prelates and popes. The discussion of the relationship of faith and works we defer to a succeeding chapter.

Like the entirety of this earth's population Martin Luther was a man of flawed character, perhaps not even the most Christ-like of the great reformers, an honor more easily bestowed upon William Tyndale. His influence in the world of Christendom and his exploration of the nature of the relationship between the Savior and His believer remain of incalculable value. Once when threatened with the punitive power of the Roman Catholic Church and its attempt to have him abandon his teachings Luther famously proclaimed, "Here I stand, I can do no other." True to his beliefs, though, like all of mankind lacking in perfection, Martin Luther has no greater epitaph than that which he pronounced for himself.

CHAPTER ELEVEN

THE AUTHOR OF CONFUSION

By the late 1500's the great reformers had passed from the scene. Those storied persons such as Wycliffe, Hus, Tindale, and especially Luther had met death, often with violence and always with a legacy. The Protestant Reformation, an historical epoch without a true beginning or a definite end had swept the landscape of Europe for decades. Its effects, both collectively and individually, were beyond enormity, and certainly with the death of its notable figure, Martin Luther, its influence did not die. Realistically, the influence of the Reformation was still far from reaching its zenith. Religiously, a new Europe, just decades previous, a basically amorphous collection of kingdoms, duchies, principalities, and rickety empires was beginning to appear with a bit of definition from the clouds of conflict. The Reformation had and was having little or no impact on the lands of southern Europe, the Latinized portion of the continent. Italy, Spain, Portugal and even the main portion of France remained resolutely, defiantly and some would say ferociously Catholic. So too did the Magyar land of Hungary, the vast dominions of the Poles in eastern Europe, and even the small island of Ireland off the western coast of Europe. The great Teutonic lands of the north, centuries before the home of the Vikings, and now Norway, Sweden and Denmark had fallen to the Protestant ideas and most particularly those of Martin Luther. Now increasingly known as Lutherans politically, religiously and culturally Protestant ideals began to dominate northern Europe and even most of the far spread lands of the Germans. Most, but not all. Northern Germany had become the strong point of Lutheranism, while the southern area of Bavaria and other provinces along the Rhine River remained resolute in their devotion to Catholicism. This religious map of Europe would remain constant and veritably unchanged for centuries until the apocalyptic wars of the twentieth century and a cultural surrender of Western ideals began to vanish in their aftermath in the late twentieth and early twenty-first centuries. For a brief moment we defer a discussion of events in England and Scotland, the influence of which may be more penetrating and lasting then anything happening on the Continent itself.

An institution as confident, self-assured and powerful as the Roman Catholic church was not about to take anything that Luther and his fellow heretics contrived in a prone posture of lying down. If a Reformation of earthquake proportions appeared so would an opposing dynamic counter to it. Although we are dealing with a certain inexactitude the date of the commencement of the Counter Reformation is often given as 1548, the commencement of the Council of Trent, wherein the still powerful church licked its collective wounds and plotted its counter to the Protestant uprising. At first basically theological it morphed into military confrontations between various "Christians" and "Christian" states, ultimately leading to the human and historical debacle of The Thirty Years War

(1618-1648), a blood soaked and ghoulish rampage through Europe, much of it fought in the name of God and His Son, the Prince of Peace. As these words are written we are some four hundred years removed from this war, or rather more properly a series of wars. To all but a few, including most historians, it is forgotten and its carcass injected with a memory vanquishing embalming fluid. Its effects, though, still linger in an age of the technological rush and artificial intelligence. But what was it?

Actually this series of wars had its starting point in Bohemia (a part of latter-day Czechoslovakia) which saw the latest episode of a dreary long running serial which had really begun in Old Testament times. Who would control the throne, political power and now religious persuasion, be it Catholic or Protestant, i.e. Lutheran. In our quick summary we will not wade into the quicksand of names, battles, generals, and generally even leaders but will offer the results of a hell-on-earth which either by battlefield deaths, famine or plague is estimated to have killed over one-half of Europe's population, a percentage not even remotely approached in the conflagrations of World Wars I and II. Entire villages and towns were destroyed, longstanding family lineages eradicated, and a legacy of fear, resentment and hatred embedded deeply in the populace. Much was done in the name of Christ, and doubtless Satan himself experienced spasms of ecstasy in seeing proud "Christians" kill each other in the name of Christ. Peace had come to Europe, but it was a tranquility that closely resembled that old adage that "... some make a desert and call it peace." In 1648 many nations, kings, princes and the various bric-a-brac of royalty signed the Treaty of Westphalia. The future boundaries of many nation states were established, but so were churches "established" in most nation states. Be they Catholic or Protestant state churches became the norm, and Christianity suffered greatly thereby, having forgotten the simple words of Jesus that "... my Kingdom is not of this world."

Europe, though, then and certainly not now, as influential as history shows it to be, is not the entire world. Neither was Continental Europe, even in the 1600's, the entirety of Western Civilization.

Twelve Miles of Water

It is a strait running a good distance of the northwestern coast of the European continent. At its narrowest width it is but twelve miles, and through the years it has been a challenge successfully conquered by many swimmers, both men and women. It separates Europe from the island now known as Great Britian, an island itself smaller than many of the individual states of the United States. Yet these twelve plus miles of the Atlantic Ocean, now known as the English Channel, has made an enormous difference in the world's history, languages, culture and most to our purposes religion. Great Britian itself is the home of three distinct peoples, the Welsh, the Scots and overwhelmingly the English. With apologies to the first two peoples our brief narrative will for simplicity's sake refer to "England."

For centuries England developed in tandem with the remainder of the bulk of continental Europe, meaning that in religious matters it was Roman Catholic to its core. Discussion of two early translators and reformers, Wycliffe and Tyndale, has already been made. Especially due to Tyndale's efforts at the time of his death in the 1500's the English-speaking world was blessed with the entirety of scripture in its common language. It remained Catholic, though the winds of change would soon turn into a hurricane, a human half scholar/half king and eventually a monster by the name of Henry VIII. His story has been recounted for five hundred years, but suffice it to say for our purposes that at least publicly he was the single most important person in moving England from the Catholic to the Protestant ranks. The change, though, was not occasioned by an epiphany of spirit but rather the libido of a king, as yet young, vigorous and of an insatiable appetite of the flesh. Henry was married to Catherine of Aragon, the daughter of Ferdinand and Isabella, the Spanish monarchs who had commissioned Christopher Columbus to journey to the new world. She was educated, intelligent, of high moral character and though a Spaniard, had become increasingly popular and loved by the English people. Henry, who would have invented the "roving eye" of infamy if it had been in place already, grew tired of Catherine and became infatuated with a young girl of no apparent great beauty but of a flirtatious nature named Anne Boleyn, whom he desired for his new wife. To summarize libraries of histories and vaults of cinema we state the plain historical sequence of events. Henry desired a divorce from Catherine, for which he needed the pope's blessing, which he refused. Henry VIII, a man of self will to equal any who ever lived, was not to be denied anything he craved. When Pope Clement VI refused to annul his marriage to Catherine, he set in motion a series of legislation in Parliament which culminated in 1534 with the Act of Succession and the annulment of his marriage to Catherine. Henry then married Anne, but now the supremacy of the Roman Church in England ceased. Henry VIII and all kings and queens to follow would now be the official head of this new church, the Church of England. Speaking of heads, the violent and vengeful made certain that those who opposed his actions, most famously Sir Thomas More, lost theirs for their disloyalty to the king's desires.

Henry now confiscated the money and much of the property of the Roman Church in England. Catholicism had been toppled from its pinnacle of supremacy, but the Roman Catholic Church was certainly not a nullity in this new and religiously modernized England. Neither Henry nor the Roman Church, though, constituted the sole influences, even secularly, in English religious matters. The English, though racially and ethnically of the same lineage and heritage as their European brothers and sisters were still different. Within the English character, often suppressed, often limited and sometimes ill expressed lay the spirit of freedom, even that of the freedom of speech and expression, which would manifest itself starkly in religious matters, especially in the century which was to come.

Slowly, very slowly, painstakingly, at times even fatally the Christian religion began to grow from not just a veritable rough debating society among popes, priests and various prelates to a possession of the common man and woman, the symbolic farm boy behind the plow so referenced by William Tyndale. In other words it began to exhibit definite signs of that which was founded by Jesus Christ Himself. To begin with the geography of England, especially in those pre-modern times, established the nation as an independent isle, one of independent spirits and though and not easily ruled by any potentate in Rome, however presumptive his title might be. Nonetheless the Church of England, or just as commonly the "Anglican Church" except for lack of a papacy highly resembled the Roman Catholic Church from which it had broken away. Many in the Church of England wished to continue in this vain and effectively be a Protestant body with a Catholic creed and worship minus the pope. This group included most of the church bishops and other clergymen. Called by many names one of those common was "High Church" and its detractors were not wholly wrong when they referred to it as Catholicism without the pope. Other groups, technically Anglicans, began to look upon church organization with a wary eye, and some were so "extreme" in their beliefs they began to look solely to scripture, not to institutional dictates nor to clergy as their guide. The names of these groups, in all honesty perhaps more political than religious, still resonate in history. They were hardly a monolithic obelisk of religion and included the Presbyterians, the Independents, the Levelers, the Puritans and many of lesser renown. The committed Anglicans of High Church were hardly driven from the field, but for the moment they did not hold the center stage. It is a priest, this time of the English Civil War(s) in which it becomes impossible to really separate the religious from the political. King Charles I, that most Anglican of Anglicans and the "wisest fool in Christendom" was beheaded in 1651, and for a time the monarchy itself was abolished. In its stead beginning in 1652 was the Protectorate, ruled with an iron fist by one of history's most remarkable men, loved and abhorred in equal shares, a Parliamentary general from the English Civil War, Oliver Cromwell. Political developments per se do not concern us, but now was a time of a Puritanical revolution in Church teachings and public morals. Church holidays, including Christmas and Easter, were no longer observed and celebrated. The high church structure of bishop upon bishop was being dismantled, ecclesiastical finery in dress was dying, and most importantly worship practices were being simplified. The teaching and observance of moral standards was becoming, well, more "Puritanical."

We will not delve more deeply into Church history in England for the moment. As important a nation and an arena for religious affairs as it was, the greater story was happening to the west. In the 1600's commencing with the Pilgrims in what became Massachusetts and the first settlements in Jamestown and other more southerly locales began the great English migration to the New World. Many, by no means all or even most, of these early colonists were Puritans who brought with them their ideas of Christianity, religious freedom (still limited but growing) and strange new ideals of government. Many, especially in the southern colonies, of which Virginia was becoming the most prominent, remained Anglican in their beliefs, practices and loyalties. Gradually, in the New World this body began to adopt a new name, the Episcopal Church. Allegiances to England and the Anglican Church, now established in England as the state church retained strength. Gradually, though, with a burgeoning population and new immigrants, the first being from the various German states, the religious complexion of the colonies began to be altered, and the number and strength of new denominations flourished with abundance.

The colonies had, for certain, their share of Anglicans, Lutherans and even to a lesser extent Roman Catholics. A political spirit drove many of these newly named Americans, a spirit that included and at times was dwarfed by a religious factor. To survive in the early colonial environment simplicity of life, manners and morals was important. With the onset of the Great Awakening in the 1700's, a general widespread religious revival, new denominations began to proliferate. Some were certainly not new, such as the Methodists, long firmly established in England, but were innovative in new and innovative ideas. This new land with greater religious freedom was fertile soil for the germination and growth of an almost infinite number of new Protestant denominations, from the already extant Methodists, he Baptists (a group that seemed to proliferate almost daily), Presbyterians, Pentecostals and countless others. They differed, as they do yet today, widely in their practices, but they shared certain commonalities. They were not Roman Catholic and all to the extent that even had such offered a worship liturgy less formal and less ornate than that of Catholicism or even Lutheranism and Anglicanism. All emphasized grace connected with faith and perhaps most importantly most emphasized a direct, even intense personal relationship with Jesus Christ, the Church's founder. They had their clergy and various church officers, but the accumulated administrative paraphernalia that had developed in the Church was diminished, often drastically so. Of paramount importance the majority emphasized the authority of scriptures, the Holy Bible, over the dictates and decrees of popes, cardinals and church councils. Some were truer to this idea than others, but most at least paid lip service to the authority of the Word. Times were changing, the New World religiously seemed marked and destined to be quite different religiously from the Old. Men and women, often simple but not simplistic, began, however imperfectly, to remove artificial barriers that had been placed in their pathways to God. No priest necessary to hear confession, no intercession by "saints" with God, and no need for self-appointed and self-important clergy to intercede between God and the Christian. The New Testament that the Christians was called by God "to boldly" come before was beginning to be remembered and recognized. To state or imply that any of these denominations or Christians was perfectly correct in their understanding of the truth certainly would be false. One of the more famous reformers (or perhaps restorers) of the early nineteenth century captured the proper attitude of the believer when he stated that:

> "We are only Christians but do not claim to be the only Christians."

As the new churches and/or denominations began to proliferate in numbers and geographic expanse across the burgeoning American landscape it became apparent that they often were quite consistent, even synchronized, with the special American character. Almost all were far more loosely organized than the religious structures from which they had sprung. Centralized authority, even where it existed, rested loosely upon most of these churches. The idea of church or congregational autonomy became a trademark of most, and again this was in keeping with the already well-developed distrust of central authority in the American character. Ministers, pastors, preachers, etc., were generally respected, although their educational credentials were probably thinner than those of colonial days in New England and the tidewater states of the Middle Colonies.

It cannot be too strongly emphasized with what commitment many of these evangelicals placed upon a one-on-one personal relationship with Jesus Christ, a principle taught with intensity by the Savior Himself. While highly educated and immensely successful individuals were by no means lacking in these churches their numbers were composed primarily of that ever ill-defined and amorphous term, the "common people." It is impossible to contemplate the membership of many of these churches without being reminded of the eloquent prayerful thanks which Christ made to His Father:

> "I thank, thee, O Father, Lord of heaven and earth, because thou hast hid these things from the wise and prudent, and hast revealed them unto babes."

Men and women in many of the "new" churches were encouraged to develop a personal, an intensely personal relationship with God, rather than relying upon the direction and supervision of clergy, priests, administrators and other church functionaries. It was the relationship which Jesus had come to establish with all, with every man and woman. The popery, the pomp, the ritualistic bric-a-brac was in many instances to be discarded to the dustbin of doctrine. The individual Christian was to be free, and encouraged, to avail himself of his personal connection to God.

Structurally and organization wise the Church in the New World came to be radically different than the Christendom of Europe. For centuries two borders had reigned in Europe, the Roman Catholic of western and southern Europe and into portions of eastern Europe and the Eastern Orthodox Church of Greece, Russia and other Slavic lands. With the coming of the Protestant Reformation of the 1500's the primary Christian body that developed was the Lutheran Church along with a few other smaller denominations. The New World began to veer in a different direction politically and religiously, and with such divergence a proliferation of denominations often too great to number and almost dizzying in their various doctrinal distinctions and differences. It is a trend that well into the twenty-first century shows no signs of abating.

In the United States the Baptist Church rose to prominence and still by almost any means of accounting remains the largest Protestant denomination, especially in the southern and southwestern regions. The religious landscape is thickly forested with so many sub-groups known by various appellation, Southern, Free Will, Missionary, American, Primitive and infinitum, at times with legitimate doctrinal differences but at other points of argument so small that they require a spiritual microscope to discover and illuminate the distinctions. This is not to point a special disapproving dagger at the Baptists but merely to offer them as an easily illustrated example of the splintering of a denomination. Others have their stories to tell, the Methodists, to some extent the Presbyterians and various charismatic groups. Perhaps even more importantly, especially in the last generation or two, a greater schism has developed, that between a more "traditional" view of Christianity and an aggressive, even secular form of post-modern Christianity, which highlights progressive and even "woke" moral principles, all of which has led to further division and even disintegration.

The modern growth of denominations in the United States continues at a staggering pace, but the growth is not of the desirable type. It has been the expansion of division and dissension, and many are disappearing from the religious landscape. More than noticeable is the realization that denominationalism is shrinking in size and influence and being largely superseded by "community" churches. The latter range from simple meeting places for worship services where the believers assemble to praise god, sometimes in a simple manner mindful of the early Church to glittering, gaudy cathedrals where various presumed clergymen, uniformly slick, slick hair, slick clothing, slick speech and a sleek demeanor preach a "gospel" which is often a strange, daresay weird mixture of spirituality and the most vulgar type of materialism. Their membership seems to be quite fluid in numbers and composition, but the line of compensation for the senior clergy often, if not usually, remains ever upward.

Almost all statistics, trends, polling data and just plain observation presently indicates that "organized" religion is on the decline in America. It is not a hide-bound curmudgeonly observation to aver that religious knowledge, especially of the nature of Christianity likewise is on a precipitate decline. Likely with more churches, religious societies, issues, media coverage, church publications than ever the impact of Christian thought, promise and morality on society seems to be more minimal than in generations, perhaps even centuries.

Doctrine, a derided word, has always had a centrality in the Christian religion. Yet, at the same time directly or indirectly doctrine, essentially "teaching" is considered too divisive to be taught in many churches, which instead substitute a fluff which ranges from social justice, progression and a "cool vibe" on the one wing to Pharisaical legalism on the other. Whatever, the Christian or would be Christian seeks from the religions buffet it is on the menu. But is this the Church, its message and the reason for being? Did the great sacrifice made by God and His Son Jesus Christ culminate in a veritable smorgasbord of religion and morality tailor-made for each individual Christian or a legalistic system of nothing more than dos, don'ts, punishments and rewards? On one extreme Christianity has been actively and even specifically defined as a legal system for which moral merits and demerits were tallied to determine the believer's fate. On the other, the predominant modern mode of thinking is Christianity as not just as a "come as you are" but also "stay as you are" system, a type of post 1960's religious thinking of "do your own thing."

For that person intrigued by Christianity and even by the already existing Christian their natural inquiry to all that has been discussed, however sketchily or inadequately for the past two chapters, lies in the realm of where he/she fits into the so-called picture. A person with but a passing interest in the Church and its history easily grasps that over the past two thousand years this institution founded by Christ Himself has gone through many changes, phases, alterations, permutations, etc., some slight and others of earthquake proportions. From a simple band of Galileans taught by the Master to a more numerically imposing group of Jews (and as yet only Jews) on Pentecost circa AD 30 to a widening to the Gentile world by the end of the first century the Church's growth was a marvel. Persecutions also grew, but the church of Christ our Savior spread to differing lands, cultures, continents and eventually across oceans. Its center, though, more and more, became not the Heavenly City but the so-named eternal city of Rome, where resided the pope, the putative earthly successor to the Son of God. Its reach, bureaucracy, riches, oppressiveness and demands of its own singularity grew apace. The individual follower of Christ was more likely to be treated as a bondservant, a literal serf, to his earthly masters the kings and princes and their religious cohorts, the flummery of the Medieval Church which dictated what each man and woman was to think and believe. Luther and other Protestant stalwarts succeeded in major efforts to teach that God's relationship to the glory of His creation, mankind, was closer and with a more intimate relationship with God than Catholicism had conceded. Then, as we have briefly noted and summarized, the succeeding few centuries unloosed an avalanche of new sects, doctrines, ideas, and unfortunately divisions. Now in what has been called the post-modern age or inaccurately (but to many skeptics) the post-Christian age what is the sincere individual believer to do and where should his/her discipleship lead. In all this miscellany of religious doctrine it is essential to remember the statement of the great apostle Paul:

> "For God is not the author of confusion, but of peace, as in all churches of the saints."

It is humanity and the opposite pole of morality, Satan, that is the reservoir of confusion. The remainder of our narrative will attempt to devote a discussion to the answer of the titular question "Am I Really a Christian." God's answer to the question is simpler than mans.

CHAPTER TWELVE

NOT OF THIS WORLD

A generally apt observation is that mankind seeks order, some type of organization to his thinking, his words, his deeds, his relationships and even his spiritual life. Chaos and confusion in any circle of life generally produce, among other items, even more chaos and confusion. Yet this is the work not of the God of Creation, but His antitheses, Satan, the very "author of confusion." A surface observation of the world, perhaps even and especially the world's religious history and life would be that on this issue at least Satan has certainly obtained the upper hand against God. The world is and always has been awash in religion, and the "Book," the Holy Bible is as illustrative of this reality as any book ever written. Especially in the Old Testament all nation's save Israel (and the Israelites by no means were consistent) were the homes of so many gods and goddesses that their numbers reached fantastic proportions. For instance, one of the most noteworthy peoples of the Old Book were the Canaanites, who by some accounts worshipped over two thousand gods and goddesses. The Israelites, the Chosen, continually lapsed into paganism, but fortunately by the time of the Advent of Christ they worshipped God only. But the cessation of confusion was but for a moment.

We have recorded briefly and even sketchily in the previous chapters the roads taken by the followers of Jesus of Nazareth from the Day of Pentecost in circa AD 30 and the birth of the very Church (the called) of Christ on that day with 3,000 Christian adherents. Simply and with an exquisite beauty did it begin, pure, innocent and the primary belief and sole allegiance of its first members being succinctly stated in but two beautiful words, "Jesus Christ." The New Testament itself is but the story of the early decades of the Body of Christ, a time of spiritual and organizational uncertainty but of fabulous growth, a time when these strange and simple doctrines were beginning to spread into faraway lands and cities, and a new spirit, the Spirit of Christ, was now a force of reckoning in humanity's affairs. Generally (but not in every instance) the Church remained united, and its growth continued apace. Our narrative, though, has noticed at least a few things that began to change and perhaps even at times redirect the mission of the Church. With the growth of numbers and the geographical expansion many Christians began to cry for more "organization," more arrangement by bureaucracy, hierarchy and that most dangerous of commodities placed in human hands, power. Little by little the Church, which after all is merely the saved or "elect" of Christ began to be enmeshed in organization, i.e. organization by geography, perhaps even culture and language and organization by power wherein various men began to assume and wield power over not but one local church but several in a local geographical district or even more, to where men were wielding strict authority and power over an increasing number of people who were literally unknown to them.

Depending upon the strength and conviction of individual Christians and the powers wielded by the church authorities, the members of this ordained Body of Christ, began to assume the character of employees or in extreme cases even slaves or serfs. The real Church power was held by Church officers, with the papacy itself at the pinnacle, and the average Church member or Christian became basically an object to whom the commanding words of the Church authorities were directed. Eventually, and the specific dates often vary with the historian this simple structure that began on Pentecost as the Body of Christ began to coalesce and form itself into that mighty edifice, part spiritual, part temporal, which dominated Western civilization for at least one thousand years, the Roman Catholic Church. By the late Middle Ages its organizational charts alone could be staggering in their complexity with so many names and appellations, some familiar and some strange, priests, nuns, prelates, dioceses, friars, monks, bishops, monsignors, cardinals and at its pinnacle the pope, the father of it all.

None of this is meant to assert that it was a slough of sin, for doubtless everywhere many members possessed the true heart and Spirit of Christ and tried to follow the Master as best they could. Increasingly and with historical existence increasing with time the Church hierarchy saw its members as mere numbers meant to be directed by their spiritual "betters." It was starting to become a very time for what we call "individualism" in either faith or politics, as the latter two were becoming interlocked and reinforcing themselves. The concept of feudalism was quickly developing in Europe by which the sovereign monarch rewarded various followers of might with lands and titles such as duke, marquis, and baron. Under each of the great lords of aristocracy, themselves subordinate to the reigning monarch, were various place holders, managers, etc., and at the lowest level were the common folk, many, if most of them serfs. While they may not necessarily have been slaves, they nonetheless were tied to the land, with little recognition of individuality and such abstract concepts as rights. They were the vast majority, their religion Catholicism, their spiritual ruler the pope and his retinue and their civil ruler, such as it was, their liege lord. They were accorded little respect and deemed basically incapable of independent action and thought, especially in any manner to their religion.

Gradually, Church discussion and theological ideas became very much a "top-down" matter, and as the medieval Church grew in geographical expanse, numbers and sheer power, both religiously and politically independent thought began to be discouraged, suppressed and stifled and ultimately persecuted. In the plainest of speech the Church leaders, the clergy, made it very clear that they would tell the adherents of Jesus Christ what to do, what to believe, what to think, and always what to give in the way of labor, goods and money, maybe not just to the Church but perhaps even more to the Church's leaders. Hopefully, these words do not convey any sense of triumphalism of a non-Catholic view over Catholicism but are mainly just reflections and echoes that many great Catholic scholars, historians and clergy have historically agreed. The Roman Church as the centuries lapsed into the late Middle Ages and the eve of modern society had grown appallingly corrupt. But – was it all bad?

The answer to the concluding sentence of the preceding paragraph is "no, it was not all bad." To a large extent and dependent upon the locale and the time Christian morality still held forth as the ethical ideal. The principal of the Trinity of God, in the Persons of the Father, Son and Holy Spirit still held great respect, acknowledgement and veneration. The great figures of the Bible were still respected as moral ideals and paragons to the point that they were bestowed by beatification with the honor of "sainthood," whereas in actuality literally each and every Christian is by definition a saint.

Not only in the spiritual but in the more temporal realms of life did traditional Catholicism act as a positive force. Artistically even the most ardent Protestant or even an atheist with any bent towards fairness would be forced to admit that the Roman Catholic Church was, for many centuries, even extending into early modern times, artistically the dynamo and beating heart of an entire epoch of history. Certainly by the Dark Ages literacy itself was becoming ever more scarce, few of the mass of the population capable of communicating by any means other than the spoken word. Literacy and learning were in full retreat, and among their last redoubts were the Catholic monasteries and much of the Catholic clergy. For centuries most of the surviving literacy works were either produced or preserved by the monks working in their isolated monasteries. Think of Beowulf in Old English or The Song of Roland, both of which were part and parcel of the early Western canon of literature. The Holy Scriptures themselves, mostly in their original classical languages of Hebrew, Greek and Latin were physically preserved by erudite and literate clergy. Unfortunately, they remained mainly in those ancient tongues until various translators and Protestant reformers began to guide the Word of God into the language of the people, in the 1400's and 1500's.

Not only with literature itself but in philosophy, theology and various sectors of the arts did the Catholic Church earn a debt of gratitude. Theologians such as Thomas Aquinas are still studied, and the fine arts perhaps most exemplified by the Italian Renaissance of the same era, and in its greatest apogee by three masters, Leonardo da Vinci, Michelangelo and Raphael.

Whatever defects and flaws that marks these men the grandeur of their artistic achievements and glorification of God cannot be denied. All were Roman Catholic. The most observable effect of what might be called the "Catholic artistic tradition" is in its architecture. Gradually the Middle Ages became the backdrop of time for the construction of magnificent church edifices across the Continental landscape and into the British Isles as well. Monasteries, cathedrals, monuments, shrines to saints, glories upon end were constructed, and most, in spite of centuries of war, are still standing. Structures such as the Cathedral of Notre Dame (actually several exist) and the entirety of the tiny state of the Vatican in Rome, the Catholic capitol and the home of such as St. Peter's Church, the Sistine Chapel, and countless other architectural wonders. Whether one is taken with architectural or artistic glories any fair-minded person would admit that they are gloriously creature, and Christians can praise them for their glorification of God and Christ. Yet therein lies a large portion of the problem.

We commence with a baseline observation that multitudes of Catholics, of whatever age, are generally good, moral persons, and that the sincerity of their religious beliefs is real. The individual moral Catholic in the persona of so many has contributed and still does so much. The direction and the organization of the Roman Catholic Church itself has always, whether with sincerity or spiritual venality been a retrogression from the simple Church established by Jesus of Nazareth. The greatest of church architecture is magnificent in its splendor and beauty, but too many have forgotten the words of the great martyr Stephen who said:

> "Howbert, the Most High dwelleth not in temples made with hands."

When the early Church began to mold the few simple dictates of Christ as to His Church's structure in the direction of man-made innovations it began a path that at its terminus is found a great apostasy from the simplicity of Christ's teaching. He is the Teacher who instructed and informed His students that God dwells not in brick-and-mortar buildings but rather in the spirit and soul of the individual believer.

Regrettably the history of Catholicism has not had church buildings, monasteries and cathedrals, as important as they may have been, as the central point of the Catholic story. After Catholicism strengthened and became a powerful force in the early Middle Ages in many lands with the lapse of time the roman Catholic Church became so powerful that it often became a partner, even the dominant partner, in a merger of church and state so close that many Medieval lands,, especially in southern Europe, were essentially theocracies wherein the head of state was not a prince, a king or even a general but the Pope in Rome. Gradually, the papacy became in addition to its religious function a potent source of political power, and the Pope himself a man who commanded more than a few soldiers, not the "spiritual" soldiers of Christ but rather soldiers who carried lethal weaponry. Historically, militarily and in legend the zenith (or nadir, depending upon one's historical proclivities) of the political power of the Pope was dramatized in a stunningly remarkable scene in 1077 in a castle located in the northern Italian city of Canossa.

In that era likely the greatest political force had become a basically ramshackle conglomeration of political entities centered in central Europe but also encompassing substantial realms in western and eastern Europe. In ethnicity it was primarily, but by no means exclusively German, and its emperor had a legitimate claim to the title of the most powerful; sovereign in Europe.

At this junction its emperor was Henry IV, a man who insisted upon the right to "invest" bishops, abbots and various clergymen with their legal and ecclesiastical authority. The Pope, one Gregory VII, thought otherwise, and a clash of titanic proportions was guaranteed. Historical and artistic accounts of all this are by no means sparse, but for narrative's purpose it culminated in Henry IV making a wintertime journey to Canossa to have an audience with Pope Gregory VII. Rather than welcome the upstart Henry, Gregory, the designated vicar of Christ, forced him to stay outside his castle and suffer in the deep snow, frigid temperatures and the humiliation of rendering obeisance to the Pope. Finally, Henry, who by this time was an excommunicant, after three days was invited into the castle, the papal ban removed and he did obeisance to Gregory as his master. Whether history totally supports the averral this is often taken as the historical and symbolic zenith of the political power of the Roman papacy, the man who was the "vicar of Christ" on earth. This, of course, is the same Christ who once proclaimed, "My kingdom is not of this world."

All of this has been a spotlight upon Roman Catholicism at its worst. History has changed so much over the past one thousand years that in few, if any, places does the Catholic Church have such a powerful grip on worldly affairs. Catholicism, whatever the locale, can still point to innumerable men and women who are sincere and even sacrificial in their beliefs. Moreover, especially in the modern era many Catholics have been in the forefront of the various battlefields wherein the clash of ideas and practices are waged, such as abortion, euthanasia, etc. Many have died as martyrs for their beliefs and have even blessed Christ while dying. Their martyrdom and principled living are never to be dismissed.

God ultimately is the judge of everyone and everything, but we are called upon to make constant religious and moral judgments, even when their airing is not necessarily pleasant. As an institution the roman Catholic Church long ago began to walk a path that would lead it into the very antipathy of what the founder of Christianity, Jesus Christ, taught. In His life and teachings Jesus, the "light of the World" illuminated every idea, thought, locale, situation, person with a light of understanding by His teachings. He daily instilled into His disciples that they themselves were the light of the world, and all their lives, deeds, words and spirit were continually to proclaim them. His apostles invited their students to examine their teachings to see if they were correct, and openly proclaimed the truth everywhere. Catholicism, though, if it is honest with itself, must acknowledge its historical record of suppressing the Word of God. Earlier our essay has noted the historical proclivity of the Roman Church to become an oligarchal institution, wherein orders and directives from on high are given, and inferiors are expected to obey.

The growth of the Roman Catholic Church in Europe roughly coincided with a darkening of knowledge and learning (hence "the Dark Ages") and literary rates among the populace dropped below the levels of contemporary third world countries. The only persons who were literate, much less with linguistic knowledge of ancient Biblical languages usually were the various church clergyman, but certainly not all of them. The Word of God was a scarce commodity as it was, but as time passed from generation to generation the great sin of Catholicism was revealed. The Church ensured its scarcity and eventually with a criminal venality put to death many of those who sought to make the Truth more easily accessible to all. The hierarchy and the priesthood were jealous of their positions, authority, often presumptuous knowledge, and they had no faith in their own membership that the ordinary Catholic could rightly interpret truth even if he held the words in his hands. As the centuries had begun to stack one upon the other so had the accumulation of religious rituals, customs and traditions that overly burdened ordinary members.

Any fair-minded observer would concede that the overwhelming majority of the Catholic clergy was not living lives awash in earthly riches. Even more so this is true for the various Catholic orders of priests, friars and especially nuns. This was likely attributable to two main factors, the first being the general poverty and the yet-developed economies in the lands in which the Roman church was prominent. Secondly, in spite of the easily noted and observable outrageous behavior of so many church officials and prelates, the majority were likely sincere servants and conscientious in their world. The government of the Roman church was the greatest manifestation of the problem, and many of its sins have provoked great comment in our present work.

As time has proceeded from Biblical antiquity through the Dark Ages, the Medieval period, the pre-modern age, modern and deepening post-modern times the rulers of the Catholic Church have always relied upon that false rubric, now as strong or maybe even stronger, that the "experts know best," even and maybe even especially in religion. This thinking and smug self-presumption that its declarant is always one of the experts is about as new as Creation itself. Yet when we believably and rightfully aver that the Roman Catholic Church's ruling hierarchy is a closed, cloistered, self-certain, and self-regarding order an avalanche of historical fact supports the assertion. Hauntingly, the attitude that "experts know best" was best illustrated by the Savior Himself, who observed the emotional and spiritual condition of the religious establishment during His own brief earthly life:

> "Woe unto you (scribes, Pharisees and hypocrites) for you lade men with heavy burdens, grievous to be borne, and you yourselves touch not the burdens with one of your fingers."

Further, they continually attacked the apostles, even Peter and John who they smugly presumed to be "ignorant and unlearned men" lacking the certification of the extant ruling authorities. With even greater searing contempt did they spurn Christ Himself because He lacked credentials and, to utter a statement of monumental truth was unafraid to think for Himself and speak His own mind.

Unlike the first century Jewish establishment which sought to slander, murder and even destroy the name, person and memory of Christ the Roman Catholic Church has always presented itself to the world as the earthly embodiment of the Spirit of Christ. Its errors in doctrine, practice and at times, many times in fact, the character of its leadership has been complex and difficult to summarize in a few words and certainly not in a singular word. Catholicism's great pitfall, though, if forced to be described in but one word is that structurally and leadership wise it became enamored with "power." Power not just in spiritual matters but earthly political power to the degree the famous eighteenth-century French atheist and philosopher Voltaire wrote advocating that mankind "destroy the infamous thing," meaning the Catholic church. Too often the institution has gained and even fostered a recognition as a forceful political power, a status which has transformed the institution into a church with more temporal than transcendent facets.

Hopefully our discourse on Roman Catholicism is not viewed as a mere diatribe, but it is intended as a fair-minded reading of history. In the name of Christ many of its adherents have sacrificed and suffered, but many have prospered and flourished at the expense of others. Now, though, we turn a discerning eye upon the question of whether the followers of Luther, Calvin and others were any better. Most importantly, though, is any of this have much, if any, to do with our titular question of "Am I Really a Christian?"

CHAPTER THIRTEEN

THOU DOTH PROTEST TOO MUCH

In William Shakespeare's famous tragedy "Hamlet" in response to some bad overacting Queen Gertrude utters a line, at least a portion of which has become immortal, "The lady doth protest too much, methinks." So, the word "protest" has been integral to the English language for a long time. It became the basis of the term commonly employed to the followers of Martin Luther, John Calvin and many others and known yet today, Protestant. Then "protested" the policies, doctrines and rules of the Roman Catholic Church and thus being protestant, a term which usage has decreased perhaps slightly in recent years. None of the great Protestant founders, though, Luther, Calvin, etc., ever referred to themselves as Protestants but rather saw themselves as reformers of the existing Roman Catholic Church. In this they failed, and Luther's followers became Lutherans, Calvin's various forms of evangelistic churches and somewhat later those of the Englishman, John Wesley, became Methodists. More notably, too, neither the term Protestant nor Catholic appear in the New and certainly not the Old

Testaments. Both Catholic (or "universal") and Protestant are man-made linguistic terminology. The New Testament generally employs the simple terms of "disciple" and later Christian to describe the followers of Jesus Christ.

The fair-minded student with a desire for an equitable understanding of other views must always balance two weights in his scale of observation and commentary. The first is truth, Divine truth, the truth set forth in Jesus Christ, the Son of God, the veritable "... way, truth and the life." Never must it comprised, but it may be studied to determine its full depths and meaning. The second weight to be balanced is a bit more prosaic. This is the requisite desire not to be haughty, self-righteous, and condemning of other's sincere differences of opinions on various subjects. Admittedly, the only person who ever perfectly balanced and exhibited these two qualities is the Savior Himself. As our essay has attempted to fulfill these goals with its discussion of Roman Catholicism a similar attempt will be made with Protestantism.

So fractured and splintered is the Protestant religious community that it is with decreasing frequency that one even hears the usage of the term "Protestant." Within living memory it is easy to recall reading or hearing presumed authoritative figures who would announce that there was extant "x" number (usually in the hundreds) of Protestant denominations in the United States alone. Undeniably, this was true, but rarely are such numbers employed today, perhaps because they have become incalculable, with religious sects, churches, etc., multiplying within practically viral proportions. Even when we acknowledge that there exist many factions, sects, schisms and divisions within the Church of Rome one organization with a vast ecclesiastical bureaucracy exists, and to a large degree Catholicism teaches doctrinal unity under the ultimate authority of the papacy in

Rome. Not so in the world of Protestantism, and it never was so from its beginnings.

In the days of men such as Tyndale, Luther, Calvin, et al., a certain diversity of opinion always existed. Still, we may find a few Protestant certainties to which all ascribed, and to some degree remain in the Protestant community. Foremost was the desirability of the proliferation of the Holy Bible in the language, whatever it may have been, of both king and commoner. The very idea undoubtedly and undeniably shifted the center of doctrinal teaching away from Rome, away from the horde of popes and priests and back towards the individual. Not only was this idea, most beautifully, inspirationally and even majestically most propounded in the English martyr, William Tundale, but also is a doctrinal replication of God's Old Testament teaching that His followers were to be a "kingdom of priests." This idea, which became and yet remains a mainstay is a God-breathed teaching that cannot be denied. The Lord's design was always to deal, to communicate and to speak openly with each man and woman. Cloaking, covering and hiding His Word behind an almost inviolable wall of priests was a spiritual abomination. For this alone men of the caliber of Tyndale, Zwingli and Luther deserve our uncompromised thanks and gratitude.

Another foundational principle of Protestantism, a natural concomitant part to direct access to God's Word, was the direct relationship of the believer to God Himself. Unlike Catholicism, wherein one could confess sins to the priest and from that point receive absolution for sin, Protestantism captured the Spirit of God, that same belief and encouragement celebrated by the apostle Paul:

> "Let us therefore come boldly unto the throne of grace, that we may obtain mercy, and find grace to help in time of need."

With this, and so much more, God invites His child to come directly to Him without the unnecessary intervention of a priest, a clergyman or even an apostle. The only person standing between God and the Christian is that one of our heart's desires, Jesus Christ. Generally this is another great principle of Truth which was deeply understood and propagated by the first Protestant reformers. Not only is it one of the core building blocks of Christianity but also it is a lifelong and growing comfort to the Christian.

In the above referenced quotation from Hebrews Paul highlighted to "grace" available to the believer. It is here, or at least was once, that a primary doctrinal distinction between Catholicism and Protestantism is to be seen. This became and remains a distinct doctrinal line between the two, and the dispute has shaped not only church matters but political, cultural and intellectual as well. At the risk of criticism for misstatement let us aver that the Catholic view of salvation rests hearty upon individual works performed by the believer and strict observance to the customs, rituals and doctrines of the Roman Catholic Church. Whether so designated or not the concept of "salvation by works" adheres tightly to such a doctrine. Doctrinally, so much of the Protestant Reformation became encapsulated in adherence to Paul's statement to the Ephesians:

> "For by grace are ye saved through faith; and that not of yourselves: it is the gift of God.
>
> Not of works, lest any man should boast."

In this one short epistolary statement to the Ephesians the great apostle employed three words which have always been and yet remain at the core of both Christian doctrine and Christian controversy. Those three words are faith, works and grace. The order of their importance, the relative weight to be given each and at times even the questioned necessity of a Christian's having all three, have been at the heart and have served as the launching point of so much Christian division. For the moment let us return to the most renown of the Protestant reformers, Martin Luther, who by his life learning and practice of his clerical duties became convinced that no person can be saved by works alone. Capable of being expressed in so many fashions any man or woman who believes that he/she may achieve salvation for eternity by sufficient good works on earth is engaged in a fool's errand, perhaps the greatest of all follies. On our own the inherent evil which we all possess becomes unmanageable and leads to spiritual destruction. Works are good. Christian works, whatever they may be, in the service of the Savior, are indicia of the submission we make and the love we have for the Master, yet their saving value is nil. So much of Catholicism has become a system of ritualized works by which spiritual merits and credits were procured. Again, in its most desiccated form it had become a veritable duplication of the hypocrisy of the scribes and Pharisees, for which so many centuries before, they had received Christ's strong rebuke:

> "The people draweth nigh unto Me with their mouth, and honor Me with their lips; but their heart is far from Me.
>
> But in vain do they worship Me, teaching for doctrines the commandments of men."

Christ never condemned works, and in fact He both exemplified them and praised them, but He did excoriate the emptiness of workers' hearts. Works, good works, good deeds, whatever they may be entitled are essential to the growth of a Christian and the brightness of his light, but on their own they are empty of value. One does not need to be either Catholic or Protestant to see the eternal vacuity of "works" standing alone. It was Martin Luther and others some fifteen hundred years after Christ's earthly ministry who began to eloquently and courageously, sometimes on the road of martyrdom, who began a chorus of disapprobation to traditional Catholic dictates on this subject.

To this ornate panoply of dead works it was Luther who began to lodge complaints and objections with increasing vehemence. Luther asserted rightly so, that works, however good and plentiful, saved no Christian, as in the words again of Paul, "... lest any man should boast." Contrary to popular belief and even much putatively learned theological opinion Luther did not deny the value of works, nor even to some degree their essentiality. His theology though, and the basis of much Protestant thinking thereafter is that real works were a growth from faith, and that standing alone good works had little value spiritually. We daresay that such an idea captures the Spirit of Christ and within it much of New Testament teaching is enfolded.

Considerate observation must now be turned to the last and most powerful of this triad of words, grace, a term that even theologically never goes "out of fashion." For two millennia mankind has attempted to define the words and frankly with even some of the more popular definitions at least a portion or essence of grace is captured. Likely still the most common definition is but two words "unmerited favor," and in our eternal context the unmerited favor is from God. Such a definition has a purity of truth, but these two words themselves raise questions of meaning. The New Testament itself recognizes that grace is capable of massive abuse, as it questions "shall we sin so that grace may abound." The scriptures place an impenetrable wall to the will of anyone who believes and asserts that grace covers all sin, all errors, all misstep for all time and can never be lost to the believer. Yet unfortunately it is not just a building block of many Protestant faiths but their very foundation.

If a question as historically and religiously huge and often complex as the primary distinction(s) between Catholicism and Protestantism may be distilled into one basic issue it is likely in the view that is taken of an individual's relationship to God. Where Catholicism has stressed the collegial and organizational structure of Christianity with an elaborate bureaucratic super structure and a hierarchical organization Protestant traditionally and in many ways has focused on the individual's personal relationship with God and with Christ. The movement now found its time, opportunity and various inchoate but developing cultural factors in the New World of North America, specifically that of the English colonies founded on the eastern seaboard on the continent beginning in the 1600's. Overwhelming the colonial settlers of the English colonies were Anglo-Saxon and Celtic natives of the British Isles and were members primarily of the Church of England, or Anglicans and eventually in America Episcopalians.

The Church in the New World

As the new "American" settlers (who in reality still saw themselves as Englishmen) began to settle the new lands of North America (and primarily for our discussion those which would become the United States) they of course carried with them not only their property, but their character, personality and beliefs. As noted for perhaps a century the settlers were overwhelmingly from the British Isles, almost exclusively Protestant and the majority of believers with still some measure of allegiance to the Church of England. Even in England, though, the 1600's were a time of almost cataclysmic change with the English Civil War, not exclusively but still in no small measure driven by violent religious disagreement, and its extended aftermath formally establishing the Church of England as a "state" church. This, though, was not the suppressive primacy of Medieval Catholicism but rather an agreement by which England would avoid further armed conflicts that had religion at their center. By now various sects, many far more committed to a Biblical understanding of Christianity had been spawned, known by many names, whether Dissenters, Presbyterians, Puritans or later Non-Conformists. Some maintained a formal allegiance to the Anglican Church, but most did not. This latter group was a great representation in the settlement of America, especially in the northern colonies, which came to be called New England. Traditional Anglicans were more represented in the southern colonies where for decades various colonial charters and governments had acceded some formal recognition to the Church of England. Only in the middle colony of Maryland did the Roman Catholic Church maintain much of a noticeable presence.

The New World was not a fertile ground for the old style established Christianity of Europe. As noted, Catholicism had but a weak and isolated presence, and Anglicanism, while more widespread, was more of a formal than a fervent religious allegiance. As in almost all lands and at all times, however, it is likely that most of the population was formally uncommitted and indifferent to matters of the spirit. Of course, by the ratification of the United States Constitution in 1791-93 and various state legislation the latter United States of America became legally off-limits for a religious establishment of any sort.

No prototypical settler came to the New World, which within a few decades became organized as English colonies and the keystone of the evolving British Empire. By 1700 settlers from different European lands, particularly Germany and Holland, began to come in ever increasing numbers. Perhaps it is no exaggeration to aver that many of them were more committed in their "Christian" thinking than even the British colonist. In the main, and their voyages to a New World so confirmed, they, both British and continental European, were more individualistic and independent in their thinking on life, both here and the afterlife. The great period of the intellectual Enlightenment had begun with so many ideas, some new, some reworkings of the old, in the fore of Western thinking. Americans (and this is the terminology which generally our text will now employ) were less prone to accept central dictates, direction or even suggestions from far away unseen, anonymous authorities in London, Rome or anywhere else. A spirit of independence was certainly requisite in forging civilization from the wilderness and fashioning a new nation, and its internal spark started to become quite noticeable, too, in their approach to the Christiann religion, its forms, litanies and morals.

Wise old Solomon once said that "...there is nothing new under the sun," and so it remained true for the early American settlers. Independence, individualism, resistance to authority, whether legitimate or unnecessarily imposed, all are certainly not novel and are replete within the pages of the Bible. Those that were religiously and spiritually inclined, seeking to become better Christians naturally were led in paths more consistent and complementary to their way of thinking and living in all realms of their lives. It was to be a long and winding road, but many Christians began to jettison the ecclesiastical bric-a-brac and spiritual effluvia of centuries that had become encrusted upon Christianity and instead seek Christ and eternal salvation through an intense personal relationship with Jesus Christ Himself. This is not necessarily because the American Christian was inherently more knowing and spiritual than disciples elsewhere, but in large measure it was prompted by his or her circumstances. Priests, pastors, ministers, etc., were not thick on the ground in the New World, and a "church" was more likely to be the assembly of a few believers in a simple structure than the large congregation in a large, perhaps even beautiful and ornate building or even cathedral with services presided over by a priest or pastor. If the disciple was literate and had the scriptures, thanks to the efforts of men such as William Tyndale, his beliefs were now formed more from the directive of the Word in its purest form, his own intellectual and hopefully the Spirit of god.

The top-down oppressiveness of the Roman Catholic clergy and even those of the more established of the traditional Protestant denominations such as the Episcopal, Lutheran, Presbyterian and others did not easily mesh with the thinking of the America Christian, particularly those of the expanding and burgeoning frontier. Although the dominant denominations which were growing with the westward movement, such as the various sects of Baptists, Methodists, some Presbyterians and others developed their own clergy, seminaries and colleges the ornate formalism of the older denominations was not as noteworthy. Greater attention began to be given to the original scriptures (or at least a lip service to the idea), and as with the Israelites of the Old Testament where every man was a priest the distinction between cleric and layman became more pronounced. A belief among many, at times even most Protestants, that the Bible was God-inspired and the sole reliable guide for the faithful Christian became commonplace, a belief which itself was an abomination to traditional Roman Catholicism. For centuries the Roman church was as solidly a monolithic force religiously as could be imagined. Its first great division occurred in the eleventh century when the Eastern Church broke away and became known as the Orthodox Church. So as not to make a diverse subject even more tedious our narrative has generally avoided a discussion of Eastern Orthodoxy. Now, though, into the 1700's and 1800's and the growth of America both that nation and culture and its Protestant ethic began a great expansion. As we have noted it was a Christianity based largely upon not the Church's institutional structure but rather an individual's own personal relationship with God and correspondingly his own personal interpretation of scripture. Existing Protestant denominations began to lose unity and cohesiveness, and the individualism of American Christians gave rise to countless new churches with their own peculiar and particular orthodoxies. Their numbers began not just to increase but to explode with a proliferation of more and more churches, a trend which has shown little sign of abatement well into the twenty-first century.

We should not be hesitant to view and properly identify the errors of Protestantism, just as this text has not been hesitant to criticize and even excoriate Roman Catholicism. The temptation is to find a pithy, even a snappy or catchy phrase that supposedly in but a bit of language that explains the perceived errors of Catholicism. Such is not just impractical, but it is impossible and even unfair to countless sincere Catholics past and present. The same may, even must be stated, for serious Protestantism, primarily that to which, rightly or wrongly, the nomenclature of "evangelistic" has been attached. Yet, in spite of our own caution and warning statements we offer the following observation. At the core of the errors of Roman Catholicism is the substitution and the exaltation of the institution of the church and its hierarchical leadership as the pinnacle of importance. At the center of evangelical Protestantism is the exaltation of the individual, his or her particular life's choices, which may in their extreme lead to the society, Biblically condemned, where every man "does what is right in his own eyes." Most definitely it contributes to false individualism and the lack of any cohesion and unity within the Church. The more individuals, the more Christian disciples, the greater the multiplicity of churches, which never seems to reach anything even suggesting a point of cessation.

The colonial idea that became the United States of America richly fertilized a cultural and spiritual soul which was already ripe for a religious, and unfortunately a sectarian feast of denominations. With a unique written guarantee of religious freedom enshrined into the founding charter, the United States Constitution, long extant denominations abounded with membership growth at a pace unseen in Europe. Numerically Methodism, already with a firm grip in Great Britain, benefited from an explosion of growth, both in churches and membership. The Baptists, while long a factor in Europe, became noted for their abundant numbers and a seeming endless abundance of sects (still a prime characteristic). Older denominations, which first appeared on the European scene in the early aftermath of the Reformation, benefited from a new locale and received a revitalization of growth. Those such as the Lutherans, increasingly a factor in America as the German and Nordic immigration rapidly increased and the longstanding Presbyterians, with deep roots in England and Scotland became a factor. It was from these same Presbyterians that a father and son, Thomas and

Alexander Campbell, gained fame in the early to mid-1800's, as they began to proclaim not reformation, but a restoration of the Church founded by Christ. They had no intention of founding a new denomination but rather of restoring the original church. With derision their followers were often called "Campbellites" but soon became known simply as the Church of Christ (of which this author is a member).

Later the Church of Jesus Christ of Latter-Day Saints, a/k/a the Mormons, was founded by Joseph Smith, himself a victim of murder for his beliefs. The Jehovah's Witnesses, a strange sect, and a combination of morality, puzzling spirituality, and just plain materialism was formed and yet exists. A roll call of the catalog of denominations, sects, and (let us be honest) cults would be tedious and too exhausting for our purposes. The cynics, and their numbers are legion, might rightfully accuse Christians, especially those of American lineage, of attempting to make every man and woman his/her private church, a temple of beliefs and practices unique and satisfying to that individual. Is this, though, the design and love of the Church's founder, Jesus Christ? A sincere believer may utter from the core of his soul the question once so beautifully and eloquently offered by the great Christian apologist, C.S. Lewis, of "... can I be merely a Christian?" Do I have any comfort of assurance with my faith? Do god and His Son provide clear lines of demarcation with the world and clear, indisputable answers to the titular question:

"Am I really a Christian?"

CHAPTER FOURTEEN

ROADS TO SALVATION – CATHOLIC, PROTESTANT OR GRACE

The United States doubtless is the most "churched" nation in the entire world, whether in its past or present versions. In many cities and towns in this huge country a walk or drive down many thoroughfares and avenues reveals an endless array of edifices dedicated to the worship of God. Especially is this of vast reaches of the South, the Southwest and large sections of the Midwest, the first two named regions for generations being referenced, often contemptuously, as the Bible Belt. These are the meeting houses, the buildings, the cathedrals of an almost infinite variety of churches, many of which have been cited repeatedly in this book. They include the Roman Catholic, Lutheran, Methodist, Presbyterian, an endless medley of Baptists, Pentecostals, Mormons, Nazarenes ad infinitum. They often differ in doctrine and dogma, sometimes in the most fair-splitting ways, but in some fashion, and to greater or lesser degrees, all (except those of a decidedly post-Christian progressive stripe) will represent that in some way the Spirit of Jesus Christ resides within the building and the worshipers who regularly frequent it. In sketching these thoughts and observations we admit to no disbelief in the sincerity of the worshipers. Strangely, though, for the overwhelming majority of these churches they share a strange, almost eerie, commonality. Almost all church names omit any mention or reference to the raison d'etre of their existence itself, its founder, the Son of God, Jesus Christ. Of course, no fair-minded student would be so stunted in his/her belief that the mention of the name Christ itself is a guarantee of legitimacy.

Still, the question arises as to why in Christendom is there often so little mention of Christ Himself. The other side of the coin is that essentially all Christian divisions and denominations contain the word "church" in their nomenclature. Church is the English translation of the ancient Greek word "ecclesia," which simply means the "called out." Many would blithely dismiss such a stated questioning concern with the almost flippant response of "what's in a name." Perhaps, but perhaps not. The very nomenclature of many churches stirs a raised eyebrow to a serious Christian, theological student and sincere seeker of consistent spiritual center. The Church is the one institution which its founder, Jesus Christ, promised would survive the ultimate destruction of the world, as He assured that "... heaven and earth shall pass away but My words shall endure forever." Remarkably, and when contemplated with serious analysis breathtakingly so the very structure, the "forever" institution is only accorded a reference to its Founder's name in a distinct minority of instances. Many churches, with somewhat impressive histories of their founding and history, pay only a silent, at times even a begrudging gratitude to their Founder. Oten they are named for men, weak, fallible men, even such as the Lutheran Church for Martin Luther or various branches of Calvinism for John Calvin. They are named even for countries or theological, perhaps even philosophical movements, as exemplified by the Dutch Reformed Church, a once potent theological force. Catholicism itself proclaims its universalism by its name, the Methodists by their one-time supposed emphasis on theological methodology and the Baptists for their presumed attention to baptism. None are disrespectful nor are they blasphemous or sacrilegious of themselves. But where is Christ and/or God and why are they such a small minority in the titular catalog of supposed Christian denominations?

We are fallen beings, and even the best of men and women when they open themselves to their own selfish nature can run astray of the humility of the Savior. From Eden forward mankind has expressed and lived a distinct proclivity to exalt himself, even in the naming of the Savior's blood-bought Church. For discussion (and essentially for reality) we see two basic elements in the Church which Christ founded. The one, the first, the lodestar of its existence is the Head of this body, Jesus Christ, the Son of God. Without Him no Church would have come into being, but because of Him and the incomprehensible love and sacrifice of both the Savior and His Father to this head has been added the Body of Christ, His Church. The body of the Church and its head, Christ, are in no sense in Heaven or on earth a dichotomy, but were designed by God Himself to work together beautifully. At times past and present certainly they have. Often, though, the self-exalting nature, the lack of humility, has touched the lives of many otherwise good, admirable disciples. Even in the naming of the Body of Christ, or as the scriptures tenderly proclaim the Bride of Christ, has humanity often, maybe even most often unthinkingly, asserted its collected ego and vain glory in the naming of the institution.

Of course, just the name Christ or God does not assure its legitimacy, but the true Christian sees comfort in being publicly a part of "Christ."

Names, words, terminology, philosophy, theology denominational and doctrinal conflicts without a seeming end have marked and stained Christianity from the beginning. Obviously, this is repellent to multitudes of people, whether they are good, bad or even indifferent to the message of Christ and His saved, the Church.

Names have an importance and Christ must ever be honored, but the name alone does not make a real Christian, nor is it sufficient, rightly or wrongly, to be the ultimate defining point of a Christian, that is a real Christian. The historical teachings of the church and its emphasis on the spiritually essential versus contrived trivialities is more important, and hopefully some of the importance of these teachings, their strengths and at times their fallacy have been captured in this extended essay. Whereas the Savior was precise in His declaration that there exists but one path to God and it is through His Son, i.e.:

> "I am the Way, the Truth and the Life;
> No man commeth to the Father but by me."

The path of destruction is not singular. It is not to Christ ad Heaven that a multiplicity of routes found but rather to Satan and Hill.

Times, cultures, persons, etc., change and ever such will be, but two basic paths of error are taken and have been historically since Old Testament days, two paths that portend to lead to God but have bitter front even as their earthly rewards, not to mention eternity. The religion of the Jews at the time of Christ's brief earthly ministry in the first century AD had much to recommend it. An apparent strict adherence to the Law of Moses, the teachings of the prophets and a reverence for their past generations were among the hallmarks of first century Judaism as taught and practiced by the Jews, God's chosen people. Yet, Jesus had the temerity, the power and the truth to point out that in reality it was a mighty edifice built upon foundations of men's, not God's ideas. The Jewish leadership, be they Pharisee, Sadducee, priest, scribe or otherwise were suffocating in their oppressiveness of the common Jewish people, many of whom were sincere in their attempts at righteousness. As the Messiah boldly proclaimed, they taught for doctrines the traditions of men and bound upon the people "burdens grievous to be born." All the while the ruling clique enriched themselves with money, material, prestige and the favor of their Roman masters while simultaneously not touching the burdens which they lay upon others. Of course, no one recognized the true heart and spirit of the Jewish religions hierarchy when He remarked:

> "The people draweth nigh unto Me with their mouth, and honoreth Me with their lips, but their heart is far from Me."

To express this in the plainest vernacular of any era Christ simply recognized that they talk a good game, but offer no real action in service to Him. As our work has suggested this is a fate that gradually befell and characterized the Roman Catholic Church. If any religious body could ever be rightfully indicted for teaching their own doctrines in the guise of Divine truth such accusation must befall the Church of Rome. Regularly have they convened in various forums, in church councils, meetings of cardinals, papal-directed assemblies ad infinitum to determine their current interpretation of a contemporary version of Divine truth, vaingloriously "... teaching for doctrines the commandments (and traditions) of men." For certain the Catholic church does not have the spiritual and mass grip on infinite numbers of Catholics in America. In Europe, the religion's birthplace, a twenty-first century post-Christian modernism has descended upon the continent, and as a proportion of the population the percentage of believing practicing Roman Catholics is at its historical low ebb. Again at the risk of sounding almost like the mimicry of a parrot we repeat that this does not blacken the hearts and records of countless numbers of Catholics who have an adherence to their traditional faith and continually display lives enriched by good works. It is a repetition of a life and spiritual scenario which was common among the Jewish populace at the time of Christ's earthly sojourn.

Our study has offered the historical gigantic figure of Martin Luther as the first man who garnered fame and real historical traction for his opposition to the tyrannical and anti-scriptural teachings of the Roman Church of his day. Of course, there were, as has been noted, many others, but it remains Luther who stands most prominently. Luther himself, a man of considerable self-confidence and self-assurance was the first man, for at least a millennium, who gained fame for disputing that a real Christian is not defined by the pope or by the Roman Catholic establishment. A real Christian is defined by the religion's namesake, Jesus Christ, who offered ample testimony and instruction as to what this means. So, is that true Christianity and the true Christian found in the admittedly disunited and confusing world of Protestantism.

Protestantism from its birth in the 1400's-1600's was never as meticulously organized nor as stultifying as Roman Catholicism, yet in its original form and its most famous divisions it was lacking in neither hierarchy nor organization, and even in liturgy and ritual. For certain the Lutherans themselves and especially the Anglicans maintained an intense level of organization and became highly involved politically, both denominations and their doctrines assuming a centrality in wars of the day. Unhesitatingly it must be averred that political involvement in the affairs of the day has never added glory to Christ and His Church and never has it been an emblem of real Christianity.

At the time of the founding of the English colonial world in the 1600's, Protestantism was in its early childhood, but its founding principles often extended centuries back to the New Testament. As referenced earlier the authority of the Scriptures was at least theoretically paramount to these early dissenters from Roman Catholicism. Early in their history, though, the various Protestant churches found that scripture itself would be subject to endless, seemingly infinite in number and variety, of construction and interpretation. A consensus of agreement, though, was essentially found in a couple of basis spiritual principles, expressed in a variety of ways but still subject to a commonality of agreement. Most importantly was and is the rightful exaltation of grace, God's gift to humanity, as the sole, irrefutable, unchanging means of eternal salvation. It was a reaction to a Catholicism that had surveyed the road to Heaven and found that any man or woman who chose this route progressed only haltingly by short, halting steps propelled by the subject's works. The Protestant reformers, most famously Martin Luther, found this an appalling perversion of the beauty of the Divine gift of salvation. Catholicism had come to teach and with a heavy hand spiritually and at times physically the precise idea of salvation which was condemned by Paul who proclaimed:

> "For by grace are you saved through faith; and not of yourselves: it is the gift of God.
>
> Not of works, lest any man should boast."

Salvation is not, never has and never will be in this fallen world by works, and in this the great Protestant performers were in the right.

No difficulty exists with the Divine concept of grace, because it is just such, a gift from God. It has been humanity's interpretation of grace wherein lies the problem and an ever-present source of contention.

Grace is not an easy gift to accept, and perhaps with the sincerity and seriousness of the Christian does a certain resistance to such a wonderful gift increase and intensify. Too often many sincere Protestants have effectively hedged their own arguments on the completeness, the perfection of grace, by wedging into their case the idea, rarely spoken in these words it might be, that the Christian, still a sinner must continually receive a new infusion of grace in some manner, often by a renewed public confession in Christ, a renewed repentance from his sins, a pledge to be better and either a direct or at least a tacit declaration to "lead a better life" and perform more good works to re-attract the Lord's attention, love and ultimately the desired salvation. The author himself, who by no means rejects the teachings and examples of the church and its traditions in which he was reared recalls a continuous feeling, a push, a prod to earn God's favor by more good works, with sadly, even tragically grace being either in the spiritual background or being uncast in the Christian's life. This was and is wrong.

Remaining is that question wrestled with by Christendom for ages, from the time in which Jesus of Nazareth walked in

Galilee, through the development of the monolith of Roman Catholicism, the Protestant Reformation and to the present, which the spiritual naysayers have called the post-Christian age. How do I, desperate for life's meaning and denying that death means eternal oblivion obtain this marvelous gold covered, platinum plated prize of "grace," by which I obtain eternal Heavenly bliss with God and Christ themselves. Men, often brilliant men endowed with marvelous linguistic and persuasive gifts have pondered, written and propounded with sincerity and wisdom on this question for ages. While it may be phased in beautiful, soaring philosophical and theological language we must concede that such is the thinking methodology of but a few. More, plainly and as this work has been titled the question that devolves into the minds of most Christian believers is "Am I Really a Christian?" Without a follow through phrase an even more bluntly expressed phrase is "can I know that I am saved and going to Heaven."

CHAPTER FIFTEEN

GOD'S ANSWER

Since its founding of the Day of Pentecost some two millennia past men and women have searched, often with an intellectual and spiritual desire which is searing in its intention for the answer to a question, posed in so many ways, but one of which is the title to this book. The emotional impetus behind the question is really that which was offered by Job many hundreds of years before Christ when he asked, "If a man die shall he live again?" To the believing Christian the positive certainty of that question's answer has been provided by the empty tomb, the Resurrection of Jesus Christ some two thousand years ago. Concern, though, should and in fact is not limited to the Christian believer alone because only a complete fool dismisses from his thinking all questions of eternity which follow that last breath which all of us take. Our own present lives upon which most of humanity has always focused its thoughts, are those of sentient beings whose earthly senses will be buried in the grave.

Yet before we attempt to provide more specific answers to any of these admittedly weighty questions, we beg the reader's leave to introduce into the discussion one final term, a word of staggering lasting and monumental importance. It completes the trifecta of words which for two millennia have been the focus of so much attention and argument and the first two of which, grace and works, have received considerable attention in our discussions. The third word is faith, a concept so huge in scope and depth and in essentiality that it is a part of the very life systems of both the Old and New Testaments.

To define "faith" is essentially to explain what the word means in all its significance and vastness. Deeply analytical and brilliant theologians have expounded deeply upon its meaning, evangelists and teachers have proclaimed, at time feverously its foundation importance, an element of Christianity which to many reduces all other Christian traits, attributes and virtues to less than their otherwise presumed importance. Luther, the great Reformer, found. Luther wrote volumes and made fierce, perhaps even ferocious, arguments for its importance, but perhaps nowhere and by no one was the centrality of this belief in faith better expressed than when he wrote:

> "Jesus Christ, our Lord and God, died for our sins and was raised again for our justification.
> He alone is the Lamb of God who takes away the sins of the world, and God has laid on Him the iniquity of us all.
> All have sinned and are justified freely, without their own works and merits, by His grace through the redemption that is in Christ Jesus, in His blood.
> This is necessary to believe.
> This cannot be otherwise acquired or grasped by any work, law or on merit.

> Therefore, it is clear and certain that this faith alone justifies us.
> Nothing of this article can be yielded or surrendered even though heaven and earth and everything else fails."

We walk on thin ice where we try to reduce any great idea, movement or epoch of history to one singular paragraph or statement, but still we offer that with the underscored phrase "... faith alone justifies us" Luther announced the pith and marrow of Protestant doctrine, and the great German theologian was quite consistent with scriptural doctrine.

Faith is defined in the New Testament as "... the substance of things hoped for, the evidence of things not seen." This definition, as famous as it is, in certain ways is unpretentiously modest. Evidence for faith may not be immediately apparent or visible but remarkably to the believer it is soon and often readily apparent. Faith is ever exalted and no more than by Christ who distributed spiritual compliments not necessarily sparingly but with precision and exaltation of the believer. To the woman with the long-time issue of blood and the Roman centurion with the servant at death's door, both of which the Savior blessed with miracles, He reveled in their faith, a faith at a level He had rarely, if ever, seen. As essential to the Christian walk as is faith, though, Luther and his legions of religious intellectuals and sincere disciples that have followed his teaching, it alone is not the eternally immutable key to salvation and Heaven. No less a figure than James, the younger brother of Jesus of Nazareth, wrote plainly in his epistle that "faith without works is dead." A Christianity built on faith alone may be purely exemplary of Protestantism, but it falls short of pure Christianity.

Historically, of central and often seemingly paramount importance in the two-thousand-year history of Christianity is the proper hierarchical value of this triad of faith, works and grace. Recognizing the generality of this assertion, subject to an abundance of qualifications it may be averred that Catholicism at least in its traditional pre-modern forms over-emphasized works, especially as such term was defined by the Church itself. Protestantism often and yet still stresses faith almost to the theoretical and sometimes the real exclusion of works. Both sectors of Christendom acknowledge grace, but generally their theological definitions of the word are not necessarily in agreement.

We have likely devoted too much thought, space and attention to such terms as Christendom, Catholic, Protestant, evangelistic, pope, priest, minister, etc. Attempts have been made to fairly amplify all of them, without slander or defamation of any sincere individual. With full apologies to the writer of the great Old Testament book of Ecclesiastes "... let us hear the conclusion of the whole matter." Suppressing those aforementioned terms coined by men let us now focus solely on the unchangeable, immutable and intrinsically understandable words of God and of Christ to answer that ever fateful question "Am I Really a Christian?"

The Holy Bible is not a book of theory but rather an extended chronicle of history and declaration of fact, or what is otherwise known as truth. It expends little time and space in debating the existence of one God, a God who is the source of Creation, of love, of everything but evil. Certainly scenes of skepticism and mockery are interspersed throughout its pages, but plainly it proclaims God's existence from the outset with the simple sentence of "In the beginning God created the heaven and the earth" and ends thousands of years later with the impassioned plea of "Come quickly, Lord Jesus." The Bible mocks the unbeliever, the atheist, the agnostic, and nowhere more starkly than one of its most famous heroes, David, proclaimed that "the fool has said in his heart there is no God."

Those short four books we call the gospels rarely proceed far in their narratives without Christ's proclaiming His joy when He encounters a believer with great faith. It is an indicia to the Son of God that such a man or woman is on God's side and impliedly yearns for an even closer relationship. Faith in Jesus Christ as the revealed Son of God, the Redeemer, is essential, a sine qua non to further proceeding down the Christian walk. Yet many very intelligent and astute observers, including much of the traditional Roman Catholic Church, certain Protestant denominations and a group or two that are identified as Protestant but themselves abjure that designation, contend that faith alone saves no one. To faith must be added works, good, plentiful, abundant works that continually grow in significance and effect to evidence a person's true Christian sincerity. Wholeheartedly and rightfully do they adhere to and praise James's ringing admonishment to "... show me thy faith by thy works." It is so easy to condemn multitudes of good, sincerely moral Christians by that dreaded term "legalist," when in many cases they are primarily interested in keeping Christian faith from becoming nothing more than a nodding assent to the Divine.

Yet how do we define Christian works, saving works, the expected works from any and all Christians? If it is possible to have a dead faith, a belief that reduces God to an abstract Being to whom a modicum of obeisance is given, it is logical to opine that works too, though they still be works, may have an aura of spiritually individualized death around them. In plainer language, if faith, apparently exercised and proclaimed in the words of the believer so might also be works. In actuality, "dead" works may be just as common or perhaps even more plentiful than dead faith. Naturally it is the Savior Himself who has provided the most illumination upon this subject. Continually for three years He walked among friends and fanatically committed opponents both, and both recognized and proclaimed the hypocrisy of the day's religious elite, usually the scribes and Pharisees. Once He even called them "whited sepulchres" who shone beautifully in the noonday sun but inside were full of the bones of dead people. They would set forth an elaborately detailed work program for the common populace but touch not a single burden with one of their fingers. At times even the good which they did was heatingly excoriated by Christ, who recognized that the motives behind their "good works" were shallow, hollow or in some cases even in venal. Exemplary of this is the incident at the Temple when Jesus commended an impoverished widow for giving but two pennies to the work, while recognizing that many, including the putatively religious examples of the day, while monetarily donating more, were giving of their abundance.

Without specifying any organization, church or body of people may we not legitimately question how many "good works" are commenced and performed which have their source far from the hearts of the workers. Christ pointedly noted this with His famous proclamation that "their lips praise me but their hearts are far from me." Maybe a hospital is constructed, a new medical research facility, a service facility for orphans and single mothers, all of which are "good works" in themselves., but not always the result of the founder's generosity and spirit. Certainly not all, perhaps not even a majority, but some good works are produced from mental and emotional seedbeds of self-exaltation, a desire for publicity to enhance one's reputation, or a peculiarly modern phenomenon to receive an income tax benefit. Ultimately, of course, only God is the judge of one's motives. The results of these works are still admirable, and they fall under that category which the apostle Paul was enunciated about those who preach Christ for personal gain that "... nevertheless Christ is preached."

Regrettably many good and admirable Christians become entrapped in a systemic belief that while they acknowledge they are not saved by their own goodness they pivot to the belief in the saving power of a life of ever-increasing good works, as if life itself was evidenced by a balance sheet of sin and goodness, and that which was in the majority determined a person's eternal fate. Historically this thinking was most completely and noticeably demonstrated in medieval Catholicism with its specified balance sheets of good works and sins, not just transgressions but sins of specified ranking and order.

Still it is not to Catholicism that we attribute any particular or peculiar weakness and falsity on this subject. Many Protestant denominations, especially those of a fervently evangelistic nature, proclaim and preach salvation by faith only, yet often immediately and glaringly contradict themselves in teaching and practice. So many of these churches have a staple doctrine of "once saved, always saved" but still continually at all sorts of services their members are exhorted to come forth and "be saved" and pledge their lives to Christ. Many good persons, spiritually minded persons, thus make a mockery of their own beliefs by having to be recharged with a new salvation when they extol as a virtue and foundational doctrine of their faith "once saved, always saved." Likely in reality many who subscribe to these beliefs, whether admittedly or not, doubt their eternal efficacy and still seek salvation by doing more works.

The disciples and would be disciples of the Good Shepherd may engage in what we have called self-mockery, but we will not add to the confusion and the misery of self-questioning spiritual uncertainty by mocking them with additional taunts. They are experiencing what seems almost endemic to the Christian believer and enjoying not the fruit of the Spirit which is God's gift to the disciple but rather the ever lurking, poisonous monster of self-doubt, a gift of Satan. This self-doubt in the grace of God and its extension to the conscience of the believer is a plague, which rots the soul and steals happiness. It is Satan's special gift, and he employs it brilliantly and with great profusion. A famous historian once focused his thoughts and words upon a noteworthy young general from the early stages of the American Civil War, the Union commander General George B. McClellan, who at the tender age of thirty-five was given command for a short period of the entire Federal Army. McClellan was handsome, energetic, of superior intellect and an organizer of unparalleled brilliance, who fashioned what eventually became the War's winning army. He possessed an undeniable charisma which still shines forth from old photographs and was generally loved and admired by the soldiers of his own army. For all his undeniable gifts McClellan ultimately proved a battlefield failure. So many were certain of his ability and he projected it himself, but a perceptive observer, the aforementioned historian Bruce Catton, remarked that with all his abilities, his plaudits from men and so much apparent self-assurance, even bravado, at key moments he would be attacked by his own fears and self-doubts, as though a denying voice were whispering in his ear "... but are you sure, General, are you really sure?" General McClellan has faded somewhat into the shadowy obscurity of history, but the self-doubt which plagued him is a Satan-induced bacillus which enters the bloodstream of many Christians and prompts the question "am I sure, am I really sure, that I am a Christian bound for a heavenly eternity."

As the conclusion of this work is approached the author wishes to slip his self-imposed traces and occasionally speak in the first person, from which I hope to propagate ideas and beliefs with no particular authority other than my own conscience, observations and experiences. The enemies of Christ and His Church from its inception and likely until Judgment easily lapse into tired, worn-out accusations that Christians are really just hypocrites, performing a lifetime's worth of religious theater to "... be seen of men." Beneath the smoothly crafted exterior lie impure hearts that pulsate with the same temptations and sinful desires as the non-believer. This Christian becomes deluded by his own self-righteousness, and his real desires are not for the blessings of God but rather for the plaudits of other men and women. These Christians are the modern incarnation of the New Testament scribes and Pharisees whose opposition to Jesus was so deep and bitter that it resulted in His death. The "Christ follower" is actually the embodiment of the hypocrite, and he employs his reputation and purported "good works" for various nefarious schemes. To all this the response is "guilty," but guilty only for a distinct few Christians.

From infancy, childhood, youth, the prime of life and into the advancing years of age I have been not "around," but sometimes even surrounded by Christians. I have observed in so many Christians various character weaknesses, improper motives and occasional pretense in life. My first target of observation is seen in the mirror, but my eyes and life's experiences have encompassed far more than this. Most Christians of a serious mindset are immensely better persons than they credit themselves, and that fact alone is strong evidence of the legitimacy of their intentions and the goodness of their character. The Church's founder and our example in all things, would have it no other way. Deep in the Old Testament lies the proverb

"Let another man's lips praise you." Modesty, moral modesty, not only honors a Christian but is the very spine of his or her character. The continuously self-assertive person, even to the point of obnoxiousness, is exemplary to other Christians and the worldly, but exemplary in the negative. This is no recent observation or phenomenon, for God recognized the general proclivity of Christians to downplay their worth and their standing. His great apostle Peter wrote to fellow Christians in the first century:

> "You are a chosen generation, a royal priesthood, a holy nation, a peculiar people; that you should show forth the praises of Him who hath called you out of darkness into His marvelous light."

Most certainly modesty is one of the greatest and even most important Christian virtues, but modesty to the point of pure self-abrogation is dangerous and in it one can even sense the possibility of spiritual self-destruction.

No decent, conscientious loving mother or father wants to see the child dispirited, downhearted, totally lacking in self-confidence and ever critical of himself and even his siblings. Yet this seems to be traditional state for many brothers and sisters in Christ's Church. Likely a cause, if at times even the major cause of this difficulty is our professed attitude towards Christian works. An almost endemic element has always darkened the thoughts of so many Christians and even of the Church itself. It is expressed explicitly or implicitly in so many ways and subject to being expressed in numerous manners. Articulated in so many ways ultimately it comes down to this, a phrase, an emotion, even a statement that "I can never do enough." Rarely is it expressed in such stark terminology the realization deepens within the psyche, and the soul is that many Christians, whatever we say, preach, teach, or feel (or at least so try) is that we are saved by our own efforts, Biblically "saved by works." Many Christians, often the most sincere, pure and morally dedicated, habitually dwell in a moral shadow of doubt and ever have before them that dread question of "have I done enough." The answer, without equivocation or exception is "No." It is not within mortal man's capabilities to save himself or herself, no matter how good, estimable or admirable it may be.

Sadly in the Church of Christ our Savior, the Good Shepherd, the Bright and Morning Star, an unacknowledged tradition, perhaps even an unknowing one, is that we as Christians are always in the debit side of our spiritual account ledger. I have no exact tabulation, yet the number is great of the instances where I have heard good Christians remark upon a man or woman's decision to become a Christian, that "now the hard <u>work</u> begins." Within this pronouncement or words of phraseology of similarity is a lack of understanding of God's true plan of salvation for his creation, man. It contains within it an absence of any importance of faith in Christ and a total disregard of grace. Sadly and mistakenly is an explicit over-reliance jupon a Christian's ability to "work" himself to Heaven and to God. Neither is it an afterthought to remark as far as hard work is concerned, without doubt we must acknowledge that Christ has already done the hard work, and we are His beneficiaries.

I cannot recall a minister, a church leader or any Christian of whatsoever standing ever coldly remarking that "we are saved by works." Yet by strong implication and inference many Churches have long taught such. Works are indispensable to the Christian life, and any such life lacking good works is resistant to the definition of Christian. They are so important that James remarked "... show me thy faith by thy works." Faith is undeniably foundational to the Christian walk, but faith alone, if we pardon the usage of a construction metaphor is like a large concrete slab, the unset concrete having been poured, carefully smoothed and treated and then... nothing. Faith is essential and often very impressive, but without works it quickly wears thin.

Taken in isolation and incomplete form our current text might be interpreted by some as a diatribe against works. Its intention is the opposite, for Christ and later His apostles, often spoke of works but did so within the content of having a strong faith as a foundation. As with almost, if not all, matters the Savior has a different approach and modus operandi than even the best of men and women, and for knowledge and salvation's seed this is what we now explore and hopefully illuminate with a bit of lucidity.

The Holy Bible is a book of immutable moral principles, codes of conduct by which a person's character is to be formed and fashioned for additional, continual growth. The zenith the very apotheosis of such is found in the short life, ministry and teachings of Christianity's founder, Jesus of Nazareth. By no means is this offered as exclusive but His most famous lesson, most oft quoted, is the Sermon on the Mount and its principles are best and most interestingly taught in almost forty fascinating stories known as the parables. Christ came to this world not to be a second Moses, a new lawgiver with an elaborate code of statutes and regulations. He came to give none of this, but rather to give Himself. Almost, perhaps in a way even all, that He spoke and demonstrated was addressed to two principles, how I should conduct myself towards God and how I should conduct myself to my fellow man. As that previously quoted scholar of the Sanhedrin, Hillel, once remarked "all the rest is mere commentary." Our Savior is perfection itself, yet He remains to humanity somewhat of an enigma. His apostle John said that the world itself cannot hold all the books which should be written about Him, but simultaneously He is capable of often being describable in but one word, be it perfect, love, sacrifice, etc. His life and teachings, though, are capable of being described somewhat more simply, and such a description is now offered.

Jesus remains completeness and perfection and without hesitation or fail He always offered Himself as proof. His character was and remains perfect, the Bright and Morning Star, the one to be emulated in all matters. Without Him our own characters can never be complete, but He taught that we should strive to always be like Him, from whom all blessings flow. The Spirit of Christ literally lives in a Christian and is seen in his/her own character. That Spirit produces fruit, i.e. the "fruit of the Spirit" as earlier cited from Paul's letter to the Galatians.

No person can be saved by works as works are generally defined by us, i.e. those acts of charity, benevolence, sacrifice to God and to man for which we feel a certain compulsion to perform. Good and worthy as they are, the salvation comes not from their performance. Works without faith is death, and faith without works is dead. Because we are weak and short-sighted our definitions of these two words are so narrowly constricted as to reveal that their explanation is from man and is human-centered. So often, and often uncanningly "faith" as we define it has a way of impliedly complimenting and praising the "faithful" for his/her intellectual and moral achievement in accepting and believing God. Too often it may be presented as almost an action or work generated within our reasoning capacity and moral prowess in accepting God's Word. This is good, but it can easily without our notice jettison the childlike wonder of the faith of certain believers who encountered Jesus in His person. We have noted the faith of the Roman centurion who knew that Christ could heal his servant with just a word of consent, the beautiful faith of the woman impoverished by twelve years of sickness who knew she only had to touch the hem of His garment to be cured and even with an inexplicable wonder the belief of the Roman centurion at Calvary who glorified God by exclaiming that "... truly this man was the Son of God." It is such exemplary faith in these and countless other persons which for two thousand years have led such hearts and souls to the Savior whom they "put on in baptism" and become "one with Christ."

From the soul and the residing indwelling Holy Spirit of God that give rise, at times almost, if not actually so, to the development of real works, that outgrowth, the fruit of the Spirit of which Paul preached. So simple, pure and unfettered with worldly complications are these works that again we recite them, as love, joy, peace, long suffering, gentleness, goodness, faith, meekness and temperance. These are the true works of the Christian character and are the seedbed of more, endlessly more and varied works by which a Christian serves God. From that character works naturally flow as does water from a nurturing stream or the coolness of a well. These works are the "living water" of which Christ spoke and gave so abundantly to the troubled Samaritan woman at the well. These are the works, uncounted, untabulated and so often unnoticed even by the Christian who is filled with the fruit of the Spirit. Certainly Christ was especially fond of this metaphor for He once taught that "... he who gives a cup of cold water in My name shall in no wise lose His reward." These are the works of which Christ spoke and with the nourishing soil of the faith, the soil from which they spring and grow, provide the true beauty of a Christian character.

Our extended essay should never be taken as an extended diatribe against an organized program of Church work. Many persons, even Christians, work best under external direction and much good may be accomplished by such organization. Let us be honest in a way that Christians rarely are with each other. To some Christians, perhaps more than we can imagine and acknowledge, too much organization is a stifling of their spirits and best intentions. Not all persons even Christians, do their best and most prolific work when they are nameplates in a congregation's organization work. To employ an old rural allusion and metaphor some persons do not work well in harness. They are not fully resistant to direction but see themselves as more securely bound by the yoke of Christ, which Jesus Himself described as light and its burden as easy. The works of all Christians, extrovert or introvert, "organization man" or independent, by whatever temporal personality description are a shining light, a light to God and that light which Christ said should not be hid under a basket but seen by all people.

For so many Christians, maybe even a majority, it is that burgeoning Spirit of faith in Christ which centers his/her life and leads to all sorts of good works which glorify God. To perform works simply from a kind of spiritual or congregational dictate is to miss the point entirely. Works come from character, and the true beautiful Christian character is that evinced by the fruit of the Spirit. This is pleasing to the Master, to God and is a true gem, a star in the crown of the faithful Christian. God thinks on so much more than we and on far higher plateaus and mountains, and so must His pleasure and happiness be likeness. The faithful Christian who manifest the fruit and the works of that faith is a Divine delight to God. Still, he/she has not attained salvation at any point on this route by his own footsteps. The sad, irrevocable and undeniable truth is that no man or woman has within their souls and lives either the ability to save themselves or even to obtain the credentials for salvation. Faith alone is dead. Works are not saving, lest, as the scripture proclaims, "any man should boast." Every man or woman on Judgment Day on the right side of the Savior will be standing there for one reason only, the grace of God.

Grace, that most important substance, idea and gift in the totality of the universe from divine inception forward to endless bless for the redeemed is impossible for present temporal earthbound men and women to fully define. Yes, we have mentioned it often, described it, feebly attempted to cloak the idea with definition, yet the stark reality is that as yet it eludes our grasp. No conception better fits the apostle Paul's hauntingly beautiful description that:

> "For now we see through a glass darkly: but then face to face: now I know in part but then shall I know even as also I am known."

"Know in part" Paul stated, and how deeply appropriate is that remark. The Christian feels, senses and should even be assured of salvation through the almost mystical agency of God's grace, but out feeble attempts at its definition are unsatisfying. Maybe we should reckon that at least in part this is prompted by our being incapable of seeing its eternal panoply. Always, it has been an accepted truism that the gargantuan monuments of frozen mass in the North Atlantic Ocean are revealed only to a very small degree, i.e. the fabled "tip of the iceberg." Generally ninety percent of these awesome ice structures are hidden beneath the ocean's surface, removed from the gaze of mankind. So must it be with grace. Of this beautiful gift we know some very salient points, i.e. that it is not earned by works "lest any man should boast" and that it is bestowed as a gift because no man or woman has ever earned or merited God's love. The source of that love, of grace, of salvation itself, lies within the heart and character of God. We see and benefit far beyond any merit by His love, a love that extends so far as to prompt the horror of the sacrifice of His only Son.

The sinner, who because of Christ's blood is no longer a sinner but a Christian, must only obey the Savior's simple command of faith in Him, a turning from the degradation of the world, the cleansing of baptism and then the joyous acceptance of God's grace. Although no theologian, no priest, no minister, no Christian of any sort would so aver often salvation by grace has been treated in the fashion of a wonderful present which God has given his beloved child, but still a present with strings attached. You may have and enjoy it, the parent assures the child, but at the first sign of conduct eliciting my disapproval it will be withdrawn and held in abeyance until you once again prove yourself worthy of it. This is not intended to be sarcastic but is rather, I believe, a fairly, dare we say, fatally accurate reading of how some Christians perceive God's grace. Most definitely grace may be lost, but the entire tone and tenor of the scriptures suggest such loss is either the intentional fall of the Christian or the adoption of a grossly negligent conduct and lifestyle. The "security of the believer" is not just a slogan, but is the reality of the relationship between Christ and His followers. Usually without or with a minimum of self-realization the character of a Christian grows and brightens with greater illumination throughout the course of his/her life. We may rightfully inquire "why should it not?" If the Spirit of Christ dwells within, effectively meaning that Christ lives within the conscience and soul of a Christian it would be a sharp anomaly indeed if that person were not better at the end of his Christian walk than at the beginning. An old, famous yet still beautiful hymn proclaims "He leadeth me, O blessed thought..." Yes, He is, through thick and thin, rain and sunshine, heartache and euphoria, abundance and poverty. He ever leads and He, the very powerful and beautiful definition of God's grace, leads from within.

CONCLUSION

Wise old King Solomon began his final admonition in the Book of Ecclesiastes with the oft quoted truth:

> "Let us hear now the conclusion of the whole matter;
> Fear God, and keep His commandments: for this is the whole of man."

Anyone familiar with Solomon, the presumed author of the above, knows that his own life was a long and winding road of danger, destiny, pleasure, almost matchless glory, wisdom and more though and along paths of temptation and sin on a level which only Satan would find glorious. Although he himself had authored much of his life's disappointment he realized his failure at the end, taught his subjects and the centuries that followed that true wisdom is found in the simplicity of obeying God. Solomon, for all his wisdom and glory, never saw or knew Christ. What a contrast between the honored King of Israel and we Christians who not only know Christ but have his Holy Spirit dwelling in us.

As this present narrative is concluding I confess that its text itself has been a long and winding road, touching about the works of the flesh, the fruit of the Spirit, comparative Biblical examples and even a very brief history of Christianity, so brief and sketchy that is bettered tagged with the name summary. It is the author's hope, though, that it has never lost sight of the necessity of providing an answer to the titular question of "Am I Really a Christian?"

From Pentecost to the present the history of the Church's founding, its early persecution, growth and apostasy has been approached. That lengthy period of over a millennium in which the Roman church, claiming a monopoly of belief, has been examined. Then followed the great Protestant Reformation of the fifteenth and sixteenth centuries, clashes of Christian beliefs and ultimately the splintering of disciples into an endless array of churches, still extant today. Since the later period of the classical Enlightenment the saga of Western civilization concentrated its focus primarily on men of science, the astronomer Galileo, the great English scientist Sir Isaac Newton, the Frenchman Blaise Pascal, part mathematician/part theologian and so many others. In our post modern (some would say post Christian times) with Western culture effectively having lost its luster among so many self-styled intellectual and opinion makers even these greats have faded a bit. But what about the religious thinkers, the theologians, the men of the Reformation, the Renaissance and even some later generations, men such as Luther, Tyndale, Calvin, Alexander Campbell and a panoply of others? They were great thinkers, admirable, courageous, but not perfect men. Their ideas, or rather their re-discovery of Biblical ideas began to lead humanity back to the early Church, founded by Christ Himself, a Church of simplicity and the gathering of the saved.

Mankind, at least in part, has always and still seeks its proper place with his Father, his God and his Savior. We Christians have had many bright lights to guide us along our life's path. No man and not even the Church is the source of salvation, and if we measure ourselves by men and institutions even the sincere heart will be restless. We desire fervently and at times with the fervor of desperation the "peace that passes understanding" of which Paul spoke. Christians in their ways, words and manner ask, "how deep must my faith be" and/or how man works must I perform, or with the melancholy eloquence of the rich young man who encountered the loving Savior, "what lack I yet?"

Salvation comes not from works, not from faith, however defined, of any level of intensity and neither does it come from Church membership, as important as these qualities remain. Almost as important as salvation itself is our self-knowledge of our condition. Christians, including this author, since the Church's founding have agonized and at times literally wept over self-doubt and as to whether the answer to the question of "am I really a Christian" is truly yes. To borrow Solomon's phrase let us hear now the conclusion of the whole matter, and its herald is the source of salvation itself, Jesus Christ. From His love, His blood sacrifice and the believer's obedience the Christian becomes just that, "a little Christ" and is saved for eternity. It was none other than the Savior Himself who is His majestic Sermon on the Mount pronounced "by their fruits you shall know them." True faith in Christ and the Father produces that exquisitely beautiful "fruit of the Spirit" of which Paul wrote. The Christian man or woman who possesses such character, a matter we hope has been adequately discussed in this narrative. That faith, the fruit of the Spirit, automatically engenders in its possessor the conduct and works so pleasing to the Redeemer. This Redeemer, our Savior, is He who is "... the same yesterday, today and forever," and His disciples are His fruit. Their eternal abode and residence is with their Savior, where they remain forever.

www.ingramcontent.com/pod-product-compliance
Lightning Source LLC
LaVergne TN
LVHW050621100826
845148LV00011B/1672